CREATE WEALTH
& ABUNDANCE IN
8 SIMPLE STEPS

About the Author

Glenn Harrold is a professional hypnotherapist and author of a successful range of self-help hypnotherapy CDs. His CDs have sold over 400,000 worldwide, and are well established as bestsellers in the UK. In 2005 the BBC released six brand new hypnotherapy CDs by Glenn on the BBC audio books label.

Create Wealth and Abundance is his first venture into the world of self-help book writing. He has written from a place of real understanding having made a personal journey from struggle and failure to great success.

If this book helps you to achieve your goals please feel free email Diviniti Publishing telling us of your success.

Glenn Harrold can be contacted at:

Diviniti Publishing Ltd
P.O. Box 313
West Malling
Kent
ME19 5WE

Telephone:	+44(0)1732 220373
Fax:	+44(0)1732 220374
Email:	sales@hypnosisaudio.com
Websites:	www.hypnosisaudio.com
	www.glennharrold.com

CREATE WEALTH & ABUNDANCE IN 8 SIMPLE STEPS

Take the 8 practical steps and learn life-changing techniques that enable you to achieve any goal you set yourself.

Glenn Harrold
MBSCH Dip C.H.

Free in this Book – Create Wealth & Abundance Hypnotherapy CD

Track One – A powerful 30-minute hypnotherapy session to help you release any blocks to success and create unlimited wealth and abundance in your life.

Track Two – A 15-minute hypnotherapy session designed as a short booster session.

Published by Diviniti Publishing Ltd
P.O. Box 313
West Malling
Kent
ME19 5WE

First published 2005 © Glenn Harrold, 2005
The moral right of the author has been asserted.

ISBN: 1-901923-79-7

Printed and bound in Great Britain by: Butler & Tanner Ltd

Cover design: Charlotte Pinkham – www.friskywhiska.co.uk
Front cover photograph: Rob Tompsett – www.rtphoto.net
Book design: Stonecastle Graphics Ltd – www.stonecastle-graphics.co.uk

I dedicate this book to:

My wife Aly for being a huge positive influence and for always being supportive and believing in me. My friend and office manager Marie Williamson for her words of encouragement and enthusiasm after reading my first dodgy draft of this book. Sue Wroclawski, Lindsay Pullinger, Fiona Davies and Claire Ellis who make up the lovely ladies at my Diviniti Publishing office. To my special son Lee who helped to motivate me when he entered this world and who always makes me feel proud of him. To my Mum, Dad, and two brothers Andy and Paul, who put up with me for the first colourful twenty years that we were caged together! To my ex-wife and close friend Kim, who has always been a voice of stability and encouragement to me and a brilliant mother to our son. To the good people who work for Diviniti Publishing in the USA and Australia. Finally, to Charlotte Pinkham who designs all my tape, CD, book and DVD covers with real love and care.

Contents

富財 繁榮

足富 運氣

幸福 幸運

Introduction

How to Use this Book and CD

Welcome. I sincerely hope that the information in this book will set you on the road to great success. If that is what you really want, all you need is a little diligence and determination. The chapters that follow lay out the principles to abundance in an easy-to-understand way so that the book has a broad appeal as I believe *anyone* can create success in their life if they have enough desire.

Throughout this book there are a number of self-hypnosis techniques and visualisation scripts designed to help you focus on specific issues. The aim of these scripts is to help you develop techniques that you can adapt for your own needs. While the CD will empower you in many areas, it is generalised and will not cover everything for everyone. There is no need to learn the scripts word for word; they are simply guides to help you go into deeper states of consciousness and reach your goals.

When you start to use self-hypnosis do not worry if you feel you are not going deep enough. Affirmations and visualisations are a remarkably effective re-programming method, even in the lightest trance states. They will still make a big impact on your inner thought processes. Just by closing your eyes and breathing deeply and really focusing on the affirmations as you say them you will begin to make quantum leaps forward. It is important to do this regularly as the key to absorbing new patterns of behaviour is compounding.

The more you use the CD and practise self-hypnosis, the better you will get at absorbing suggestions. Focus on one thing at a time until you feel you are ready to move on to the next goal.

The CD enclosed with this book provides a powerful hypnotherapy session to help you to create success and abundance. It has been designed to compound the content of the book and so I suggest that you listen to the CD regularly while you are reading the book, and then use it to reinforce your ambitions and goals any time you feel the need. The CD will help to free you of any personal blocks to creating abundance and success. Believing that you have a right to abundance and success is the first and most important step you will take.

The book guides you through a number of steps to creating abundance and success. It begins with an outline of my journey from want and struggle to abundance, and I reveal the key elements that helped me make that leap in a short space of time. You will also learn many self-hypnosis and visualisation techniques to help you reframe your beliefs and achieve your goals. The information you absorb under hypnosis will have a powerful and lasting effect. It is completely safe as you will be guiding yourself, and deciding on your own goals and aims. These methods are extremely effective and will teach you how to draw out your true potential and achieve almost anything you set your mind on.

Seeing the Possibilities

If you are reading this book while you are a resident of the UK, USA or most other western countries, then you live in a place where incredible abundance and opportunity are available to all. Even if you live in a poor area, or have little money, it is possible for you to change your circumstances and become wealthy in a short space of time. I'm not saying it will be easy, but with a bit of knowledge, some new positive programming and a little hard work, financial success can be achieved by anyone.

The first and most important factor in becoming wealthy is to have belief. If you believe that only others become wealthy or that you don't deserve to have money, then you will have little or no chance of achieving success. Most people's inner beliefs about money hold them back and stop them from achieving any sort of abundance. Yearning and longing that you could be rich is a waste of energy and essentially counter-productive. You have to flip out of any such mindset, change destructive, negative beliefs and take consistent, positive action towards your goals. You need to create a thought process whereby every cell in your mind and body believes that you are rich *now* – even if your bank statement says otherwise! Create the belief first and you will soon manifest the reality.

> *"Your vision will become clear only when you look into your heart.*
> *Who looks outside, dreams.*
> *Who looks inside, awakens."*
> Carl Jung

Most people spend far too much time and energy trying to *save* money and not enough *making* money. When you learn to focus all your energy on making money, gaining wealth becomes much easier: you stop wasting energy worrying about money or feeling there is never enough. The key to success is in developing a positive outlook, and my aim is to get you to overcome negative obstacles and help you unlock the door to abundance and wealth. Once you pass through that door and learn the secrets of abundance, your life will change in many ways.

However, becoming rich will not be a panacea for all your problems. Wealth brings new concerns. Most wealthy people worry about how to keep hold of their riches and how to sustain their lifestyle. You also face the dilemma of wondering if some people like you just because you are loaded. The other problem is keeping your stash away from the taxman, who is always keen to relieve you of chunks of your wealth.

In recent times I have experienced these concerns, which can be a bit of a downside to abundance. However, in my younger years I experienced living in a council flat in a rough area with little money to survive on. I know which situation caused me most stress. For me, having no money meant having no freedom, having to do many things I didn't want to do and having to spend time with people I didn't want to be with.

Having money enables you to experience life more fully and take more control over the way you live. I would say it is crucial in experiencing life to the full. That is not to say you can't be happy if you are poor, as there are many people the world over who are happy and get by on very little. However, in the western world there are more opportunities to become wealthy than ever and so why not focus your energy on joining the rich club? I really don't buy into the idea that you can't be a good person spiritually if you are rich. Money is totally neutral; it is how you use it that counts. Money is simply an exchange of energy. If people use their wealth to control or to manipulate others, then they are using money in a negative way and become corrupt as a result of their own greed or bloated ego. I guess that is where the saying comes from: "Money is not the root of all evil; it is the love of money."

> "Money is totally neutral; it is how you use it that counts."
> Anon

I think it is healthy to step outside our comfort zones now and again. On the journey to wealth and abundance there will be times when you are faced with big dilemmas and you will need to make bold decisions. Experiences like fire walks, glass walks, sweat lodges, parachute jumps, or bungee jumping can be great for boosting self-esteem. If you walk across burning hot coals or jump out of a plane, it leaves you with the feeling that you can take on any challenge in life. I once took part in a sweat lodge*. It was an all-male affair that took place at the top of a hill in remote countryside, on the day of the winter solstice. The temperature was zero degrees, and we stood naked as the day we were born, with freezing wind whistling around our parts, while a short ceremony took place. Then we spent four hours in a tent, exposed to intense heat from hot granite stones creating a sauna-like effect. There were about ten of us involved from all walks of life, including a couple of middle-class white-collar guys, a few ordinary working men, some new-age chaps with dreads and a couple of your typical tree huggers. The idea of a sweat lodge is to break down barriers between people and to connect

---

* A sweat lodge is a Native American Indian ceremony that involves small groups of people entering a tent or tepee. Hot stones are then passed in and placed in the centre of the tepee. The heat can become intense and the length of time spent in the sweat lodge can run to many hours. The aim is to cleanse the body of toxins, the mind of negativities, and to heighten the spirit.

you with your inner spirit. I found the whole experience to be great and felt a lot of respect for everyone involved, as it was quite an ordeal to spend so long in a muddy tent in such intense heat. As part of the ceremony inside the tent we each had to ask for one thing and meditate on this as a personal goal throughout our time at the lodge. One of the chaps asked for more compassion, one asked for greater knowledge, another for happiness. When it came to my turn, I asked to become financially rich.

My goal was greeted with mild amusement and opposition from one or two who thought it was "not spiritual" to make such a request. I couldn't understand this and was soon embroiled in a lively debate. I pointed out that when I became rich I was going to use it for good, to help people and to experience life more fully. I honestly believe that having money has helped me to develop my spirituality and has made me a better person. There is no better kick for me than being able to help out a friend or family member who needs a financial leg-up or to donate spontaneously to a worthy cause that touches me. As a result of my abundance I've employed other people and helped to give them a steady income; I've also travelled around the world and have become more knowledgeable and enlightened as a result. Now, pray tell, what is "unspiritual" about all that? There is no exclusive spirituality in poverty.

Never let others hold you back. If you believe that being rich is a positive thing, and that it will improve your journey through life, then go for it 110 per cent if that is what you want. You will need to keep your focus on money and success for much of the time, but that is fine; just make sure your journey to success and abundance is an honourable one where you make decisions with integrity and honesty. There is no need to trample on others to get to the top; there are a million-and-one ways you can become rich and empower others as you do it. Even in the world of stocks and shares, ethical investing is becoming increasingly popular. There are huge investment funds that only invest in companies that are doing something positive in the world. Companies that damage or pollute the environment, or are deemed to be unethical, are excluded from these funds.

There will always be characters that use their money to control and
manipulate others, but that is life. There is nothing *unfair* about
dishonest tyrants becoming wealthy. Creating abundance is equally
available to all of us, even the mad and very bad. There are always a
few rotten apples in the barrel, and in life you always make your own
choices. The secret is to enjoy your money and to make it work for you.
Don't let money rule you or become the most important thing in your
life. Keep your ego in check at all times, even when others get excited
and impressed by your wealth. An out-of-control ego has caused many
a millionaire to implode!

My Story

I have put many of my own experiences into this book and I hope my stories will help to motivate and inspire you.

My early years were very challenging and I had to overcome more negative programming than most, as my teenage years were traumatic and very unstable. From the age of 12 I spent many freezing-cold nights sleeping rough on the streets and at 13 began drinking heavily. I had run-ins with the law and was involved in many street fights. On one occasion, when I was 16, I was beaten up so badly by a gang of ten lads outside a bar that I was left unconscious and later admitted to hospital with concussion. During the same year I lived on a gypsy site for a few weeks as I had nowhere to stay and a couple of gypsy brothers kindly put me up in their caravan. That was as rough and ready as it gets. My heavy drinking culminated in me contracting hepatitis at 17, and I was told by a doctor that if I did not quit drinking I would be dead within two years. I also got into all sorts of mind-expanding drugs, which I took in excess up to the age of 20. In short I was "fucked up" and I sometimes wonder how I am still reasonably sane. The point is, if *I* can turn all that around and create success, then so can you.

On the positive side, my upbringing helped me to become a knowledgeable therapist, as I learnt about most problems through life experience, not just from a textbook. I believe that some of the best therapists are the ones from troubled backgrounds, as tough experiences can give you real understanding and empathy for people who are struggling. Once you are out of the woods yourself and free of self-destructive patterns caused by negative conditioning, it becomes possible to teach other troubled souls how to free themselves from their problems. We sometimes learn the biggest lessons in life through adversity, and experiencing difficult times certainly gives you more compassion for others.

When I first became a hypnotherapist, many of my clients were kids brought for therapy by parents who wanted a solution for their child's "bad" behaviour. I found that the problems almost always stemmed from the parents' dysfunction, and that the kids' behaviour was a product of their environment. Some of my most successful therapy sessions have been with so-called problem kids. Whatever their presenting problem I had usually been through it myself.

One such successful session stands out in my memory and demonstrates the untapped potential that many of us have inside:

An anxious mother once brought her troubled daughter along to my clinic for therapy as a last resort. The 16-year-old was on the verge of getting expelled because she was dropping out of school and had lost all interest in lessons. Her exams were ahead of her and her mother was frantic with worry. I was able to build a good rapport with the girl and over three or four sessions helped her to resolve many inner conflicts. I felt the sessions had gone well and that she would have a new positive focus on her schoolwork.

Two months later the girl called me in floods of tears. She had just got her exam results and had achieved incredible results, beyond all expectations. She had got eleven straight A$^+$s, and was the top girl in her school! The tears were tears of joy and she told me that her success was all down to me. In truth it wasn't as she was a bright girl. My skill was in reframing her outlook and bringing out her potential.

The story is a good example of what can be achieved with hypnotherapy. We each have so much talent and brilliance inside us; every single one of us has unique abilities and infinite creativity. The key to success is in learning how to connect with our unique inner potential and to draw it out. The techniques, ideas and teachings in this book will help you to do just that.

Eight Steps To Wealth And Abundance

Take 8 practical steps to create great wealth and abundance in your life and learn life-changing techniques to enable you to achieve any goal you set yourself.

▶▶ Free yourself from any blocks to abundance!

▶▶ Learn the key universal laws of abundance!

▶▶ Develop powerful new inner beliefs for success!

▶▶ Learn self-hypnosis techniques to draw out your creativity and potential

▶▶ Take the 8 practical steps to create great wealth and abundance in your life!

▶▶ Learn life-changing techniques to enable you to achieve any goal you set yourself!

Step 1 – Opening Up Your Mind to Believe that Anything is Possible

Cutting back on Excess

If you are mortgaged up to the hilt and stuck in a job that is limiting your potential to the point where it is hard for you to jump ship, I feel for you. I really do, as I have been in this position and worse, and I know how frustrating it can be. In my early twenties there was a six-month period when I often had bailiffs knocking at my door, and I was once just 24 hours away from having my tiny, two-bedroom, terraced house repossessed. I had county court judgements against me, and high interest building up on payments on loans. I felt totally trapped. It took me years to pay off my debts, and the experience taught me a hard lesson: do not spend money on goodies if you can't afford them.

You may feel totally seduced by the idea of having that groovy new plasma wide-screen hanging on your living-room wall, but if you can't afford it, the stress of paying back the loan will soon outweigh the pleasure you get from having it. Debt is debilitating and will stunt your journey to abundance; so you may need to cut back and loosen your financial constraints.

> *"Never spend money before you have it."*
> Thomas Jefferson

I learnt to do this only after my brush with the bailiffs, when I made a personal vow never to get into incapacitating financial straits again. I disciplined myself to buy luxuries only if I could afford them and I steered clear of borrowing. Some people spend more than they can afford just to impress others or to keep up with their upwardly mobile friends. If you are guilty of this, then you need to free yourself from any such bullshit and let go of the greed that drives reckless spending, especially when you can't afford it.

Behaviour like this is purely ego-driven anyway and it is not the true path to abundance. To achieve financial freedom and start to spend your money for the right reasons on things that you can afford, you need to subjugate your ego's needs and whims. There is nothing wrong with blowing ten grand in one day on a shopping trip if your income can support that, but if you are earning only £300 per week, then you need a completely different approach to spending. So get into the habit of living within your means and stay free of any non-essential borrowing.

> "Don't go around thinking the world owes you a living. The world owes you nothing. It was here first."
> Mark Twain

Your starting point must be to cut back on any excesses. Live minimally if needs be, then you can start to breathe and focus on achieving abundance.

Another good starting point is to clean out any clutter from your home so that you create a feeling of having more space. Maybe sell any possessions that you don't really need anymore, as this will help to put a few readies in your hand. I really like the idea of minimalism and have got into the habit of taking any clothes I haven't worn in the last six months to the local charity shop.

Try not to get too attached to personal possessions and instead focus on creating a healthy flow in your life where there is an "easy come, easy go" feeling. As much as we may enjoy having many fancy luxuries, we can't take them with us when we depart this life. So think of them as things you enjoy for now but accept that one day you will let them go. It is important to free yourself from over-attachment to material possessions.

Creating the Belief

Creating positive new beliefs is crucial if you are to succeed on your journey to creating abundance. It is a good idea to view this as a journey as you may have a few ups and downs on the way. Most millionaires endure many failures before they hit on the success trail. We hear only about Richard Branson's successful ventures, but he had a few failures before he made his first million. The only difference between Branson and most would-be entrepreneurs is that he never gave up, and just kept going and going. His business achievements should be a real inspiration to all wannabe millionaires.

We all deserve the best, and there is more than enough money sloshing around in the world for the spread of abundance to create many more millionaires. There are also many more opportunities for everyone to make money today than at any previous time in history. My grandfather worked in

> "The best way to have a good idea is to have lots of ideas."
> Linus Pauling

the same factory in London for 50 years; he was on the bare minimum wage and received only a crappy watch when he retired. That was the norm in those days. He had no other opportunities for work and nor did he expect them, because if you were born into the working classes in those days there was a high probability that you would die working class. Nowadays, in the western world, people from poor beginnings can become rich and successful in a short space of time.

I didn't come from a poor background, but until my mid-30s I earned less than most guys my age and never had any savings. In a nutshell I spent those first 35 years potless, but that was the journey of a song-writing musician who never quite wrote a number one hit! However, when I started to use the principles outlined in this book I hit the abundance trail and my financial circumstances dramatically improved. Anyone with diligence and determination can do the same.

From here on I want you to accept that enjoying abundance is normal and natural and not just something that happens to a few other lucky people. You must develop a mindset where you truly *believe* that you are wealthy and that you totally *deserve* the very best in life. With strong inner beliefs you can create as much success as you desire. Make your plans clear, keep things simple and be relentless in pursuit of your goals. You will be amazed at how quickly things will change.

Summary

▶▶ **Cut back on excessive or unnecessary spending that you cannot afford, so you can free yourself of negative feelings about money.**

▶▶ **Free yourself from attachment to material possessions.**

▶▶ **Focus on the fact that you live in a world of opportunity and unlimited abundance.**

▶▶ **Believe that you can be as rich as you want to be and that you absolutely deserve to have great wealth and abundance.**

Step 2 – Releasing Negative Conditioning and Focusing Your Mind

Releasing Negative Conditioning

We are all conditioned by patterns learned from our childhood upbringing; more so than most people realise. If you had been born and raised in a remote jungle in a distant land your world-view would be a million miles from the one you have now. You would still have the same brain and personality traits but your conditioning would be vastly different. Our habits and idiosyncrasies are made up from old beliefs about ourselves, and the things that we experienced when we were growing up. Failure to recognise these patterns of conditioning is what holds most people back in life.

You need to become aware of any childhood conditioning or patterns that may be holding you back. For example, if as a child you were told constantly that you were useless or an idiot, you will actually create situations in your adult life where you end up looking stupid. On a conscious level you will hate creating these scenarios and you will probably beat yourself up even more for making yourself look like an idiot, but on an unconscious level you will be driven to continue. Conversely some people try to over-compensate for things they lacked in childhood. We all meet people who are arrogant or who love to impress, but they do this only because of their own insecurities and deep-rooted lack of self-belief.

> *"There is no sadder sight than a young pessimist."*
> Mark Twain

Unless you address negative patterns – if necessary through therapy and psychoanalysis – you will continue to be driven to create destructive situations as a result of beliefs that were formulated by your upbringing. It doesn't make rational sense to mess things up now because of bad teaching years ago but that is what happens to many people. If you have any patterns of self-sabotage that were formed in your childhood, you need to address them and then change them. The journey to abundance can be hard if you are dragging a ball and chain behind your leg. You will learn more later in this book about letting go of destructive patterns. I have always found that using hypnotherapy to regress to the root cause of problems is the best way to overcome negative conditioning. If you feel you have big self-sabotage patterns going on, you may want to consider working through them with a good therapist.

I am going to relay a case study that demonstrates how effective hypnotherapy can be in releasing negative conditioning. The gentleman in the story was totally stuck in a destructive pattern of behaviour that was destroying his life. This client called me at my clinic and said he was an alcoholic and that alcohol was destroying his life. He was desperate to be free of his drink problem but didn't know how to do it. It can be difficult to help alcoholics with hypnotherapy alone but after our telephone consultation my feeling was that I could help him.

He explained that he had been locked into a very destructive drinking pattern for eight years. He was putting away a bottle of vodka a day and had become very aggressive and abusive towards those close to him. Paradoxically, although he was seen to be a tough kind of guy, he had also become very emotional and tearful. He made a vague connection between the onset of his problems and a car crash eight years previously.

After an in-depth consultation I guided him into a relaxed state and regressed him back to the time of the accident. Under hypnosis he recalled the accident in full. He had been involved in a horrific road accident in which someone in another car had died. He was in no way to blame for this tragic event as someone else had caused the accident; this had been confirmed at the inquest. The odd thing was that although he was not at fault, he was nevertheless tormented by guilt.

I regressed him further and it transpired that on the evening of the accident he had promised his son that he would be at his school awards ceremony to see him collect an award. Instead he had worked late and would not have made it to the school in time. In his deepest thoughts he blamed himself for the accident. In the trance state he said, "If I hadn't stayed late it wouldn't have happened". His feelings were complicated and compounded by the guilt he felt about letting his son down and he had blotted out much of this painful memory. For eight years he had been unable to face the thought of what had happened and had submerged himself in drink; embarking on a violent, self-destructive lifestyle. He was basically punishing himself because he had this deep-rooted repressed guilt.

Under hypnosis he was able to remember everything and face it for the first time since it had happened. I guided him to resolve this inner conflict and release the guilt. At the end of the session he was crying and he said he felt massive relief for the first time in eight years. He couldn't wait to get home to his family "to start to make up for being such an arsehole." His words. I knew at that point that his drink problem was over. This man had seen many doctors and had shown no improvement, yet with one straightforward regression he was able to resolve this inner conflict and free himself from self-destructive behaviour.

When I saw him a month or so later he looked totally different as he had not touched any alcohol and had no desire to go back to it. He had lost weight and looked happy, healthy and full of life; so different to when I first saw him. He told me his wife wanted to say thanks as she now had her husband back.

This is a dramatic story but it demonstrates how people get stuck in negative patterns that hold them back or, worse, destroy them. It also shows that it can often be easy to overcome such problems.

In heavy cases like this, an experienced therapist using regression techniques can provide the solution. I always found *regression to cause* can achieve great results; this is because when we store memories, we store the associated emotions as well. So, if you go through a trauma and it becomes repressed, the memory and the connected emotions get stuck. If something triggers that memory years later, the emotions are also released. This can feel very confusing if you do not understand what is happening or why it is happening.

The effect of music is a positive example of this. When you hear a song that reminds you of a time when you once fell in love years before, just hearing it again can bring back the warm romantic feelings you had at that time.

The therapy content of this book, together with the CD, will be adequate to help most of you to release any poor conditioning or blocks to creating abundance.

Learning How to Focus

Maintaining your focus is a crucial part of becoming successful and you will need to develop the habit of becoming single-minded in the pursuit of your goals and aims. It is an empowering habit to cultivate. Many top sportsmen and women have learnt this skill, as to be the best in any sport you have to be totally single-minded. Top athletes often display tunnel vision and the ability to maintain high levels of concentration over long periods. In doing this they harness all of their energy to achieve a specific outcome. If you generate enough energy and focus on your goals, they will manifest. There is nothing complicated about the process; it is simplicity itself when you get it right.

> "Shoot for the moon. Even if you miss, you'll land among the stars."
> Anon

When you meditate or use self-hypnosis to achieve a goal you are programming yourself to succeed on a deep level. There is more on this in Steps 3 and 4, but for now think of this analogy. Imagine an iceberg with its tip above the water and the huge bulk below the surface. This image is often used to describe the conscious and unconscious mind. We spend most of our time in our conscious thoughts and tap into our unconscious mind only sporadically: when we daydream or get creative ideas. The only other time we spend in our unconscious thoughts is when we sleep as our conscious mind has switched off. Learning to connect with your deep unconscious mind through focus and meditation can be very empowering. It can help you in many different ways to achieve goals, develop your creativity, or overcome difficulties.

The following is a useful meditation discipline for developing your ability to focus. It is a good way to familiarise yourself with the process of going into a trance state.

Stop at this point and read the script through a few times until you know what to do and then practise this discipline for the next few days. You will find that the more you practise, the deeper into trance you will go each time, and the better you will get at it. Learning how to stay focused is crucial to your success.

Go into a quiet room where there are no distractions. Light a candle and place it in front of you. Turn off all the lights so the only light is from the flame of the candle.

Sit comfortably in front of the candle and focus on the flickering flame. Watch the movement of the flame and begin to breathe very slowly and deeply: in through your nose and out through your mouth. Make each breath long and deep, and clear away any thoughts so your mind becomes still and centred. Don't worry if you get the odd unwanted thought. Just centre your mind again and allow the thought to drift away. Focus on the stillness of the moment.

Be in the "here and now" and accept everything as it is.

Continue to watch the flame and remain centred and focused. Stay in this relaxed state for as long as you like. Ten-, 20- or 30-minute sessions are ideal. Whatever suits you. The first time you practise this mental workout focus on nothing but clearing your mind and staying centred. Don't underestimate the power in the simplicity of this as it can be a very good discipline for building your concentration.

After you are used to this, you may decide to focus on a particular goal each time you meditate. When you do, focus on one thing at a time and keep it simple. Alternatively you can use it to find solutions or to draw upon your creativity.

When you have finished, blow out the candle and close your eyes, and notice the thoughts that come to you at this time. You will feel refreshed and relaxed and you may find you get some inspiration or new creative ideas may come to you.

It is also helpful to use this discipline before you go to sleep, as it will help you clear your head of thoughts and will relax you.

Summary

▶▶ **Recognise negative patterns that are holding you back so you can work on releasing them.**

▶▶ **Learn how to develop the ability to focus.**

▶▶ **Meditate on focusing your mind.**

Step 3 – Creating your Goals and Affirmations

How Goals and Affirmations Work

A goal is a specific target that you set yourself to achieve within a fixed time frame. An affirmation is something you state or repeat to yourself over and over again. Affirmations should be words and phrases that are stated in a clear and concise way with a positive emphasis. Whenever you affirm, feel as though you are drawing the words inside you; as though you are teaching the inner part of yourself a new belief. You must always state affirmations in the present tense and focus on them as if they are a reality now.

> *"Create the belief in your mind and the reality will follow."*
> Anon

Even though you may not own an Aston Martin or whatever your dream car might be, when you affirm and visualise it is important to see yourself driving and owning it now. Absolutely believe it is real. When you focus consistently on a goal or affirmation, the image or thought becomes absorbed into your unconscious mind as a reality. Once the new belief is absorbed by your unconscious mind, you will respond to it automatically in your daily life. This may manifest itself in you consciously or unconsciously by creating situations and opportunities that bring you effortlessly closer to your goals.

Writing down your goals and affirmations is very important as it gives the words power and meaning, reminding you constantly of where you are heading. Writing also spells out your intent loud and clear; it helps to add clarity to your aims and compounds your new belief structures.

I experienced a defining moment soon after I decided to focus all my energy on becoming abundant. I'd just become a full time hypnotherapist and was helping many clients to achieve their goals and I decided to use these skills to create my own success. After some contemplation I listed many material goals that I wanted to achieve: the luxury car, the big salary, the fabulous house, the holiday home in Florida. I listed these and many more goals in colourful detail and wrote them down in the present tense. One major goal was that I would earn £5000 per week, and as I wrote it down, a negative thought kicked in, saying, "Don't be daft. How are you going to earn 5K a week when you have never even earned £500 a week?"

I realized something important at that moment: don't ever let self-doubt or negativity get in your way. Negative thoughts are a part of what makes us human, but don't dwell on them. Just let them drift away and refocus on the positive. You only fail if you give up; so be diligent and stay on course as success will happen if you devote enough energy to achieving your goals.

I pinned my list of goals next to my bed so I would see them as soon as I opened my eyes each morning. I also pinned up a picture of a brand new Mercedes convertible and another of the kind of large detached house that I wanted to live in. I then used a self-hypnosis technique to see myself enjoying this new abundant lifestyle and immersed myself in my vision so that I totally believed, on a much deeper level, that this lifestyle was a reality now. This technique serves to give you total acceptance of abundance. When your deep unconscious accepts your goal you will respond automatically in your daily life and begin to create opportunities for yourself. I meditated on my goals and self-hypnotized daily, and also listed a number of affirmations which I repeated both in meditation and during the course of my normal daily life. Not that I was chanting mantras on the train each day, but I did get into the routine of using empty time continually to affirm my goals.

It is easy to acquire the affirmation habit. For example, while in the shower or on car journeys, get into the habit of turning off the radio and repeating your affirmations instead. Make the whole abundance thing a part of your life. During quiet time is ideal, when there is no other stimulus, if only for five minutes each day. Cultivate these good habits and build them into your routines. You will be amazed at how quickly things can change in your every day life when you are resonating with this abundance vibration.

Think of this analogy. If you wanted to build your physique or tone your body you would go to the gym each day to work out. You would then make physical changes pretty quickly. The same applies to creating abundance. The more energy you put into achieving your goals, the quicker they will materialise. Most people fail to succeed because they are wishy-washy or half-hearted about achieving their goal; but if you state your intent clearly and work diligently towards it, you can achieve anything. Always remember to enjoy the journey towards your goal, as creating positive mental states on a regular basis can be fun and empowering in many ways.

Listing Your Goals

At this point I want you to list your goals on one piece of paper. Take a bit of time to think your goals through, because what you write down will become reality. Be specific, as the thoughts you send out are very powerful – so they must be clear, to the point and completely positive. For example, don't say, "I am going to come in to money" as the unconscious won't interpret this very well. It is possible to come into money by having an accident and receiving compensation.

State your goals along these lines:

I earn £50,000 per month by using my talents and creativity positively.

I will be worth £1 million pounds by the age of ––.

I own a large £1,000,000 detached house with a swimming pool.

I own a £70,000, top-of-the-range, silver Mercedes convertible.

I travel the world in style and I have complete financial freedom.

I continue to build my business into a very lucrative and profitable concern.

You may also want to add goals that are about achieving a personal aim. Here are some examples:

I make a wonderful living as a successful artist.

I earn a huge salary from playing professional golf.

I am a very financially successful musician.

I compose a song that is a hit all over the world.

I write a million-selling music CD album.

Reminder:

Whenever you reaffirm or use self-hypnosis to focus on your goals and affirmations always state them in the present tense as though they are a reality now. Your unconscious mind will then accept them as a truth and you will respond accordingly.

There is more on this in the guide to self-hypnosis section (see page 46).

It can be hard to get used to making statements in the present if you are living in a tiny council flat while affirming your salary is £10,000 a month. However, think of it as though you are reprogramming a computer with new data. What you put into it is going to come back out. You are only in the tiny flat because of poor data in the first place. Maybe your lack of belief or inaction is the problem. If this is the case and you want to change things, you will need to make some fundamental changes – and reprogramme yourself – at the deepest level.

If you work hard at changing your inner beliefs through your goals and affirmations you will soon create a new outer reality. Totally immerse yourself in your aims. When you are in a trance (see p.46) use all of your senses to compound the phrases. Make your visualisations colourful and real. I used to get so deep into my self-hypnosis practise that my wife said the bed I was lying on would often gently vibrate. I was blissfully unaware of this when I was in my deep inner focused state. I am actually not particularly good at visualising but I am able to focus well and I would immerse myself in the belief that I was rich. (See "The power of imagery" on p.51 for guidance on how to visualise.)

If you are not good at visualising do not worry as you may have a different dominant sense. Most people are visual but others absorb information more easily through sensing, feeling, hearing, smell or even taste. So it is good to use all of your senses when visualising, as your more dominant senses will help you to absorb the new belief at a deeper level.

When you reprogramme yourself in this way, you will be amazed at how your circumstances improve. The discipline is about working on yourself and being creative in your inner work. When you create powerful new beliefs, the outer reality will always follow.

Reviewing Your Goals

It is good to set a future date to review your goals so that you can evaluate your progress from time to time. Once you have created a momentum and you start to achieve success and abundance it can be easy to forget where you were at when you started. I often forget how quickly things have changed as I tend to focus on the future much of the time. I have now developed the good habit of forward thinking and making the most of new opportunities, so I rarely look back and reflect. I figure the time to do that is when I'm 90. However, it is useful to stop and take stock of things every now and again, so you avoid becoming too driven. Keeping a balance in everything you do is very important.

Balance helps you to adapt to change with ease and really to enjoy the whole abundance journey.

Once you have decided upon all your goals, set your review date. List at the top: "Goals to be reviewed on January 1st 2----", or whatever date you decide is appropriate. For long-term or big goals you may need to allow two or three years (or whatever feels right to you).

Create your own list of goals and read them every day without fail. Feel free to adapt any of my examples and elaborate on them. You might want to have another list of short-term goals, for example:

I quit my job and start my own business.

I am now running my own successful business.

Listing Your Affirmations

Once you have decided on your goals, you will need to list your affirmations. One of the first things you need to focus upon the release of any negative feelings or emotions you might have towards money. For example, if you have previously split up with a partner because of money problems or your parents used to row about money, then you may have some negative programming that needs to be released. Read through to the end of this chapter and use the self-hypnosis guide on p.46 to let go of any negative feelings you may have towards money. Once you have learnt the self-hypnosis technique use a few practice sessions to work on these affirmations.

I release any negative feelings towards money and success.

I let go of any fear of success.

I accept it is my divine right to be abundant.

I accept unconditional abundance on every level.

I deserve to be wealthy and successful.

Dealing with negative emotions

The first two affirmations above – the ones about dealing with the release of negative feelings and letting go of fear – are very important. If you feel you have issues around money that have held you back, then in the first self-hypnosis session, focus solely on letting go of any poor programming or fearful emotions. You may want to include your own affirmations or releasing technique to free yourself from some specific constraints of the past as you will be your own best therapist here. Do not underestimate this part of the process as it underpins everything you are going to build. Clearing out negative conditioning so that you can develop a positive psychological model is crucial for future success.

A house built on strong, deep foundations will withstand any kind of battering; and likewise you need to programme yourself to believe there is no hardship or lack of opportunity, and that it is easy to make money. If past programming has been destructive and is a big problem, you may want to consider a series of one-to-one sessions with a good therapist to help you move forward. However, for the majority, the self-hypnosis techniques in this book will be sufficient to free you up to lay some solid positive foundations for success.

On the CD accompanying this book I have included some post-hypnotic suggestions to help release negativity. Once you feel that you are over the negativity hurdle, you will be ready to develop your new positive abundance programme. When you work through negativity that may have previously held you back, notice how you feel about it afterwards. If the feelings are no longer negative then you can move on.

There is a way to test how positive your attitude is to wealth. When you see someone who is rich, how does it make you feel? Do you feel jealous or insecure? Or do you genuinely think, "good for them, they deserve it and I know that I will also achieve great success"? If you experience any resistance to their success then you need to spend more time releasing your negative feelings before you move on from this point.

Creating Positive Affirmations

Below are some examples of affirmations that I still use regularly. Feel free to add any of these to your own list and acknowledge that you will get into the habit of affirming your phrases many times a day.

When you state your affirmations say them as though they are a reality now.

I am always in the right place at the right time.

Abundance flows freely and naturally to me.

All of my needs are constantly met.

I deserve to be successful and prosperous.

I feel very comfortable making lots of money.

I deserve great wealth and abundance.

Money comes easily to me now.

I am generous and abundant.

I give and receive easily.

I treat people honourably.

I believe in myself.

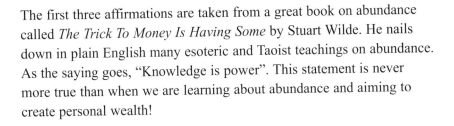

The first three affirmations are taken from a great book on abundance called *The Trick To Money Is Having Some* by Stuart Wilde. He nails down in plain English many esoteric and Taoist teachings on abundance. As the saying goes, "Knowledge is power". This statement is never more true than when we are learning about abundance and aiming to create personal wealth!

Summary

▶▶ Take time to write down a list of clear goals. Keep them somewhere where you can read them each day. Always stay focused on your goals.

▶▶ Use the self-hypnosis technique on p.46 to compound your goals on a regular basis. Visualise all your goals as a reality now, and be very creative when you visualise by using all of your five senses.

▶▶ Write down a list of positive affirmations in the present tense and affirm them in your daily life as often as possible.

Step 4 – Using Self-Hypnosis to Compound your Goals and Affirmations

The Unlimited Power of the Mind

The real power to realising your goals is inside you, and hypnotherapy is a wonderful tool to help you draw out your potential. Hypnotherapy works by bypassing your conscious, critical thought processes and accepting suggestions at a deeper, unconscious level. When your unconscious mind accepts the suggestions, you will then respond to them automatically in your everyday life. This positive programming at a deep level is a crucial step on your path to success, so make it a part of your daily routine. Building positive energy is the quickest and most effective way to create the momentum that will speed you towards success. Remember the analogy of programming a computer with positive data: what you put into it is what you will get out.

It has been said by many erudite people that we use only 10 per cent of our brain power. This quirk is unique to human beings as almost every other species on our planet use their full brain capacity. It is strange that we humans are lugging around huge brains that we barely use. However, when we develop the art of going into altered states of consciousness through self-hypnosis and visualisation we begin to tap into that larger part of the brain – the 90 per cent that is usually dormant. This vast unconscious part is where your dreams take place and where your creativity and real talents lie. Some people have a natural ability to go deeply inside through focus and concentration but it is also something you can practise and develop.

It is said that Albert Einstein came up with the theory of relativity while in a trance state: a waking trance in fact – while he was shaving! When you repeat mundane everyday tasks that take little thought, your conscious mind becomes still and you begin to access your unconscious mind. Everyone experiences waking-trance states in their daily life. For example, when you are driving on a journey that you have done so many times that you don't have to think about the route, you switch off your conscious mind and your unconscious mind takes over. You drive automatically, without thinking about the journey.

We all experience hypnosis at least twice a day, when we go into our natural state of semi-consciousness: a *hypnogogic* state before sleeping and a *hypnopompic* state before waking. Incidentally these are very good times to recite your affirmations, as you are naturally receptive last thing at night and first thing in the morning.

Never underestimate the power you have inside you. Your mind is a truly amazing thing with incredible potential. All around the world there are stories of humans achieving feats that are seemingly impossible. There are many documented cases of mothers being able to summon superhuman strength to lift a car off the ground to save their child who is trapped underneath. When the mother sees her child in danger she doesn't stop and think; "I can't lift that car as it weighs too much". The only thought in her mind is to save her child and the fact that the car is too heavy to lift never enters her thinking. Through extreme focus and sheer force of will the mother is able to summon the strength to lift a car weighing over one ton.

The survival instinct is the most powerful drive that humans possess and when this is compromised in extreme circumstances we can do things that defy logic. When we are in serious danger our focus becomes heightened and we enter an altered state of consciousness. In this altered state we can display incredible strength and power. By using self-hypnosis you will be able engage your mind in a similar way and achieve so much. Use the mother lifting the car story as a metaphor for your journey to success. Never put a limit on what you can do. You can achieve absolutely anything when you learn to focus your mind.

You can manifest amazing things through your beliefs. I know that I have repeated this a few times but that is because it is *the* crucial ingredient for creating wealth, success and abundance. Create the belief first and the reality will follow. *You* have the power within *you* to create any belief, which you can then realise through focused energy.

Understanding How Hypnotherapy Works

When you use self-hypnosis you become both therapist and client. It is therefore a good idea to plan your self-hypnosis sessions beforehand so that you can decide on a clear goal before you begin. You also need to decide upon your affirmations. There is more on this in the self-hypnosis guide in the following section.

There are five typical stages in a clinical hypnotherapy session:

1. **Introduction**

2. **Induction**

3. **Deepening**

4. **Post-hypnotic suggestions and affirmations**

5. **Awakening**

Introduction

The introduction is the building of rapport between the therapist and client.

Induction

The induction is the first stage of trance, created usually via breathing techniques, and by using exercises that release tension and stress.

Deepening

This is the guiding down into a deeper state of hypnosis. It can be achieved for example by counting down from ten to one or via many other deepening techniques. Once the client is in a deeper state of hypnosis they are more receptive to suggestion.

Post-hypnotic suggestions

Post-hypnotic suggestions are the most important stage of the self-hypnosis process, as these phrases empower, motivate, dispel fears and have a powerful and lasting effect. The hypnotherapist delivers the post-hypnotic suggestions when the client is in a deeply relaxed and receptive state. The client will then act upon them at a later date. For example, if the hypnotherapist makes a post-hypnotic suggestion that "You will feel more confident when you are in company", the next time the client is in company they will respond to that suggestion automatically, as the suggestion is now anchored in their unconscious mind.

Affirmations

Affirmations work in a way similar to post-hypnotic suggestions. They are first person, present-tense phrases that the client will affirm to themselves as a reality now. For example, "I feel confident and secure."

Awakening

The awakening is the gentle transformation from deep relaxation and alpha-state consciousness to full waking consciousness. This can be achieved by using post-hypnotic suggestions and a slow count upwards from one to ten. (For an explanation of alpha-state consciousness, see p.53.)

Learning and Using Self-hypnosis to Empower Yourself

Once you have completed your goals and affirmations I want you to learn and use the following self-hypnosis technique to focus on the affirmations at a deeper level. Use these techniques regularly along with the enclosed hypnotherapy CD, so you continually reinforce and compound your new beliefs. I have also included two hypnotherapy scripts for abundance (see Appendices), which you can adapt for your own aims.

> *"Be great in act, as you have been in thought."*
> Shakespeare

Your unconscious mind believes exactly what you tell it or, in this case, what you affirm. It won't get emotional about your affirmations or criticise them (criticism takes place in the conscious mind). When you repeat your affirmations in a deeply relaxed state your unconscious mind will accept the suggestions as a reality. You will then begin to respond to the new programming in your daily life without thinking about it. Keep blasting positive affirmations deeply into your unconscious mind and you will be amazed at the progress you make.

I have a friend who is a singer and songwriter who told me that when she learnt about self-hypnosis and the power of affirmations she would regularly affirm that she would have a number one hit. Every day she would get herself into a very centred state and affirm and visualize this scenario in colourful detail. Within one year of starting this discipline in the mid-nineties, she wrote a song with her partner that went to number one in the British charts. I have seen the gold disk on her wall! So believe in this stuff, because absolutely anything you want is just waiting for you to step up and claim it.

> *"You only fail if you quit."*
> Anon

There is a funny aside to this story. On the night she found out her song had gone to number one, she was playing a gig to an empty pub in the middle of nowhere. When she arrived she was so excited she said to the landlord, "My song has just gone to number one in the charts", and the landlord replied, "Yeah love, whatever you say, just set your gear up in the corner and get on with it."

If you spend time getting your affirmations right you *cannot* fail, as you will truly empower yourself on a deep level. Whatever practical steps you take towards abundance *never forget* to continue with your positive programming throughout. You cannot always accurately measure the effect of self-hypnosis, meditation or visualisation but I know that without the inner work much of my success would not have happened. So you need to put your faith in the process, especially at the beginning when you are working hard to get things going. This is often the hardest time as in some cases you will be trying to turn the tide of failure. However, once you do turn the tide, the momentum you create will build and speed up.

I once knew a guy who was very successful but was spiritually bankrupt and "as tight as two coats of paint" as the saying goes. I often wondered how he had managed to make it to the top, as at the time, with my limited knowledge, I didn't think he deserved success and could not understand why he always seemed to be so "lucky". One day I got into a deep

> *"Imagination is more important than knowledge."*
> Albert Einstein

conversation with him and he told me that as a little kid he had always been able to visualise himself living in a big house with a swimming pool. Even though he was a tight so-and-so, he had managed to visualise his way to success. If he had held that abundant picture in his head constantly as a kid, it was inevitable that he would take huge steps towards achieving his goal. Through his visualisations he had created a powerful positive programme on a deep unconscious level.

The universe is totally unemotional and whatever you project out there is what you will get back. This concept is an important aspect of creating success, so make sure you are crystal clear about your aims as you are going to get everything back that you ask for.

From here to the end of this chapter I explain in detail how you can use self-hypnosis to empower yourself. I also offer a brief technical explanation of the various states of consciousness. The following is a simple self-hypnosis guide that you can learn and develop. If you use this and adapt it for your own needs, you will soon get the hang of tapping into your inner creativity and talents. Once you have read the process through a few times, practise it as often as you can.

A Brief Guide To Self-Hypnosis

This guide to self-hypnosis has a wide variety of therapeutic applications. In particular it is very effective in the alleviation of stress and tension, in helping to regulate sleeping patterns and when focusing on goals.

Creating the right atmosphere

Find a quiet room where you will not be disturbed, preferably a bedroom with no telephone. Dim the lights or turn them off. You may choose to light a candle, or burn some aromatherapy oils. Use anything that helps you to create a relaxing atmosphere. Then make yourself as comfortable as possible, either in a chair with a headrest or by lying down on a couch or bed.

Preparing yourself

Tell yourself silently or out loud that you are going to practise self-hypnosis. Then tell yourself silently or out loud how long you want to remain in the trance. Fifteen to 20 minutes is fine to begin with. However, after a few weeks practice you may decide to make your session last longer.

The breathing technique

Close your eyes and begin to breathe very slowly and deeply, in through your nose and out through your mouth. At the top of your breath hold for three seconds, and then count to five on every out-breath. As you breathe out imagine you are breathing away any nervous tension left in your body.

Make sure you breathe from your diaphragm (lower chest area) and not from the upper chest. Watch what happens to your body as you breathe. If you are breathing properly your stomach will go out as you breathe in, and will go in as you breathe out. This can take a little practice if you are unused to diaphragmatic breathing.

You can also say the word *relax* on every out-breath if you wish. Continue this breathing pattern ten or more times, or as long as it takes for you to feel completely relaxed.

Clearing your mind

Allow your mind to go completely blank. Don't worry if you still get unwanted thoughts drifting into your mind; tell yourself not to fight them, as they will soon drift away again. Every time you get an unwanted thought, imagine a large red stop sign. As soon as you see the red stop sign imagine the thought disappearing and your mind becoming clear.

Another thought-clearing method is to imagine a large computer screen full of data that becomes blank by hitting a keypad. Imagine that by pressing a keypad, you can clear your mind. Another method is to imagine you are looking up at the sky on a pleasant summer's day. You notice a few small clouds that drift across the sky and then fade away. Eventually all of the clouds have drifted away and the sky is clear. Imagine your conscious thoughts are like clouds that fade away. Use whatever method works for you.

Deepening the trance state

By now you will already be in a light trance state. A good technique to guide yourself deeper into trance is to count down silently and mentally from ten to one. Feel every muscle in your body relax more and more with each descending number. Leave about five seconds between each number, or count each number down on every second or third out-breath. To enhance this you can also use visualisation techniques. For example, imagine yourself travelling down ten flights in an elevator; or stepping down ten steps into a beautiful garden. Count down with each flight or step, going deeper with each number. Use whatever feels right for you. Don't get hung up on the feeling that you are not deep enough in trance or that nothing is happening. Being in a trance is often very subtle. The more you practise, the better you will get and in time you will begin to know intuitively when you are in a deeper, more receptive state.

Conversely do not fear going into a deep state of trance, as this takes you to a powerful part of yourself where you can make big changes. Allow yourself to go deep inside your mind and tell yourself you feel safe and secure as you do this. Someone once asked me if they could get *stuck* in the unconscious state. This cannot possibly happen. You may fall asleep in trance, but you would then wake up in your own time as you would from a regular sleep state.

Utilising the trance state

When you reach the deeper trance stage you can either relax and drift or you can give yourself some positive suggestions or affirmations. The wording of these must have been decided upon *before you start*. You can also use powerful imagery (see "The power of imagery", below).

Word your affirmations correctly

Work on only *one goal at a time*, usually over a number of sessions. Don't for example work on releasing a fear and creating success in the same session. You can use a number of affirmations in one session but they must all relate to your one chosen goal at this time.

Silently and mentally repeat the affirmations over and over, slowly and positively, using as few words as possible. Be very direct as though you are giving yourself commands. Sometimes you can create a rhythm with your breathing saying the affirmation on each out-breath, almost like a chant or mantra.

When deciding on the suggestions beforehand always state them *as if they are a reality and in the present*. This is very important, as your unconscious mind believes *exactly* what it is told. For example:

Do *not* say: "I want to be wealthy and abundant."
Do say: "Great wealth and abundance comes easily to me now."

> *You must make any suggestion completely unambiguous and Always Accentuate The Positive.*

Really *feel* the affirmations as you repeat them, draw them inside you and let every cell in your mind and body resonate with positive feeling and emotion. Imagine every part of you is repeating the affirmations with complete conviction and total belief in what you are stating. Even if it feels a bit odd at first, stay with it, as your unconscious mind believes exactly what it is told. You are creating new positive beliefs that will be accepted by your unconscious exactly as they are, without any analysis. That is why taking time and care to list your affirmations correctly is very important.

Bringing yourself back to full consciousness

When you feel it's time to wake up from the trance all you need to do is slowly and mentally count up from one to ten. Tell yourself you are becoming more awake with each number. When you reach the number ten your eyes will open and you will be wide-awake enjoying a feeling of total wellbeing.

If you practise before going to sleep, you do not need to count up from one to ten. Simply tell yourself before you begin that the trance will turn into a deep, natural sleep from which you will wake up in the morning feeling positive and refreshed.

Please note

Do not worry if, when you first practise self-hypnosis, you don't feel that much happened or you could not see much in the visualisation. Just the fact that you went somewhere quiet and centred yourself by closing your eyes and relaxing will have benefited you.

You will be surprised at how effective a suggestion can be in even the lightest of trances. The power of the unconscious mind works in a very subtle way. The most important thing to remember is to enjoy the process and to have faith, because as with all things, the more you practise the better you become!

The power of imagery

Using visual imagery as well as words when in the trance state is a very powerful way of absorbing beliefs into your unconscious mind. For example, as you state your affirmations on abundance, *see* yourself living in an abundant world where you have all the riches you want. Be creative and make the visualisations colourful and elaborate, including as much detail as possible. Maybe see yourself driving your brand new, dream car. Notice the colour of the exterior and the aroma of the new interior. Immerse yourself totally in the visualisations and harness all of your senses to make them realistic.

When you visualise a future event, run the images in your mind like a short film *using as much detail as possible*. If you are going to a meeting see the shape and size of the room, notice the colours of the walls and carpet, feel your clothes against your skin, notice the fresh smell of the room, the softness as you sit in the chair. Make the whole picture bright and clear and use as many of your senses as you can; the more vividly you use your imagination, the better. Most importantly, *always see yourself in a completely positive light*, expressing yourself clearly and confidently and feeling very calm and composed under any pressure.

You can use this powerful technique to prepare yourself for so many eventualities, such as an exam, a sporting event, public speaking, for business and social occasions. I always feel for people when they blow a big opportunity through nerves or anxiety. Learning these techniques can help absolutely anyone overcome their fears in pressure situations.

Remember
Your unconscious mind cannot differentiate between what is real and what is imagined, so the more often you imagine a future situation or event in a positive light, the more you create and compound a new inner belief that you are calm, confident and in control in these

situations. When you come to experience the event in reality, your unconscious mind will believe that you have been there before, and you will feel as composed and in control as you are when you visualise it. Once again think of the mental rehearsal as a way of programming a computer with new positive information that you will respond to at a later date.

Preparing for meetings and interviews

Self-hypnosis and visualization will help you overcome any blocks to success and are useful tools for getting you in the right frame of mind for any potentially nerve-wracking meetings or interviews. If you are due to go for an important meeting and you feel nervous, practise this visualization before you present yourself for the meeting:

Use self-hypnosis to drift down into a receptive trance state. Then see yourself at the meeting feeling composed and full of confidence and conducting yourself in a very positive way. Accept that you may experience a small degree of nervousness, but understand that you are in control of the level of anxiety you feel. Use your anxiety to keep yourself focused and on the ball. Visualise the meeting from start to finish with as much detail as possible.

This type of future-positive visualisation is great for helping you to be at your best for meetings, speeches, important dates or any type of performance. I use the technique whenever I feel anxious about a future event and it works a treat every time. Repeat the process often, and on a daily basis when leading up to any big event or meeting. The bigger the event, the more visualisation preparation you should practise on a daily basis.

Hypnosis and Brainwave Function

In a typical hypnosis session your brainwaves will actually slow down as you go deeper into trance, and then speed up as you come out of the trance. This also occurs naturally when you go to sleep each night, and then conversely when you awaken in the morning. These brain cycle states are referred to as the beta, alpha, theta and delta states. An easy way to remember this is to think of the word BATTED, or to visualize a scene relating to the four trance states in which you see a ball being batted. You will remember the words much more easily if you create a picture in your mind.

Beta waves

The frequency of beta waves ranges from 15 to 40 brainwave cycles per second and is typical of full waking consciousness. Beta waves are characteristic of a strongly engaged mind. A person engrossed in a stimulating conversation would be in the beta state. In a heated debate or argument a person maybe in a high beta state.

Alpha waves

Alpha is the next state and the frequency ranges from nine to 14 cycles per second. This is achieved through relaxation or light meditation when you are still aware of everything around you but your mind is calm and you are feeling physically relaxed.

Theta waves

Theta brainwaves are typically between five and eight cycles a second. This is the state you achieve when you are in deeper hypnosis. You are very receptive to suggestion in this state. It is the aim of the hypnotist to guide the client into alpha and theta as in this very relaxed state suggestion can be given and readily accepted, and then acted upon.

Delta waves

Delta is the final brainwave with a range of 1.5 to four cycles per second. Your brain will be whirring away at a frequency of two to three cycles per second while you are asleep. The deepest hypnotic trance state is somnambulism, which occurs when you are in, or close to, the delta state.

The experience of dreaming and trance

When we go to bed and wind down before going to sleep, we are likely to be in a low beta state. When we close our eyes and relax, our brainwaves will descend from beta patterns, to alpha, to theta and finally, when we fall asleep, to delta. It is known that we tend to dream in 90-minute cycles. Dreaming often occurs when delta brainwave frequencies increase to theta brainwaves. When in between the delta or theta states we often experience realistic or lucid dreams.

When we dream deeply and vividly, rapid eye movements (REM) can occur. REM can also occur under hypnosis, and therapists often look for this cue when hypnotising their clients, as the client will be very receptive to suggestion at this point. (Incidentally, the US rock band REM takes its name from this abbreviation.)

People often misunderstand the hypnotic trance state. When you go to sleep at night and you drift between consciousness and unconsciousness, your brainwaves begin slowing down. You will also experience natural trance states in between being awake and going to sleep. Hypnosis is a similar experience. When you go into a hypnotic trance it can sometimes feel as though very little has happened. You are often very aware of your surroundings and are able to open your eyes at any point. However, your brainwave frequencies will have slowed down.

Be aware of the occurrence of this subtle shift in consciousness when you are practising self-hypnosis and going into trance states. Hypnosis is often subtle and deep trance does not occur at the sudden click of a finger despite what you may have seen performed by stage hypnotists. This type of high-profile theatrical induction is a misrepresentation and creates a false impression. In most normal sessions the induction into deeper hypnosis is gradual and controlled by the client.

Don't get hung up about achieving a certain depth of trance. Absorbing suggestion is the crucial element in therapy-based hypnosis and this can be achieved easily even in very light alpha trance states. The important aspect when you are focusing on abundance and success is to create clear, powerful, strong affirmations that you can feed back to yourself under self-hypnosis.

Summary

▶▶ **The unlimited power of the mind.**

▶▶ **Understanding how hypnotherapy works.**

▶▶ **Using self-hypnosis to empower your personal goals and affirmations.**

▶▶ **Compounding your goals and affirmations on a daily basis.**

▶▶ **Learning how to develop self-hypnosis and visualisation to help overcome anxiety and develop a positive frame of mind for any potentially nerve-wracking meetings, interviews or performances of any kind.**

▶▶ **Hypnosis and brainwave function.**

Step 5 – Setting the Wheels in Motion and Connecting With Your Creative Mind

Drawing Upon your Creativity

The next step on the abundance trail is to develop ideas that will use your talents and creativity in new ways to make money. Always remember you have unlimited talent and potential. You may not always be using it to the max, but it is always there. Use the trance state to connect with your inner creativity and talents. The creativity script (see p.60) and the enclosed CD will help you.

The quickest ways to become rich are: to marry someone who is wealthy, to inherit money, or to win it. Now these options are unlikely to come about, but you should never discount them. A woman once wrote to me to tell me she had been using my *Create Unlimited Financial Abundance* CD for just six months when she met a millionaire whom she later married. Another lady wrote to say she had been using the CD for a week when she found a scratch card that won her £1000. Both women put their sudden abundance down to working with the CD. At one time in our office we had an intense week of focusing collectively on creating abundance, with abundance symbols and affirmations written down everywhere. The following week we had all won sums of money, including a £500 win on the Premium Bonds and a first prize of £2000 in a local lottery.

These stories are amazing really and hard to explain, but I've included them so that you can see why it is good to stay open to all possibilities and never to put limitations on how abundance will come to you. It is worth adding that you should always state in your suggestions and affirmations that money comes to you under positive circumstances.

Now although it is important to stay open to any of the above possibilities, it is not a good idea to rely on them alone. You also need to take more practical action to create your riches, and one good way is to start your own business. If you have time on your hands then that is great, but many people are stuck in full time jobs where they don't have the time to start up a new business. If that is the case with you, you can begin to think along the lines of starting a sideline with big potential.

The Internet can be very useful in this area as it is not too expensive to start up a good on-line business that can become lucrative very quickly. Having a busy on-line e-commerce shopping site is like having a shop that is open 24 hours a day, 7 days a week, 365 days a year, and that can be visited by 90 per cent of the world's population. What a fantastic age we live in.

> *"The man with a new idea is a crank, until it succeeds."*
> Mark Twain

I have included a practical information chapter about the intricacies of setting up and marketing a commercial website at the end of this book.

Focusing on your Talents

I cringe whenever I hear people whine that they haven't got any talent. I believe every man, woman and child walking this planet has an abundance of inner talent to draw on. It is usually laziness, apathy or lack of belief that stops many people from finding and expressing their talents or fulfilling their potential.

Some people can pick up a guitar or paintbrush and display outstanding ability from an early age; their vocation is clearly defined from day one. The rest of us have to dig a bit deeper to find things we can do to illuminate the world and fulfil our creative desires. However, just because you can't sing naturally like Aretha Franklin, play guitar like Eric Clapton, or paint like Rembrandt doesn't mean you are without talent. You just have to go inside and dig deep and unearth the gems inside you. I also believe that if you are passionate about something, you can develop a skill for it even if it wasn't there in the first place. I have a love of writing and recording songs. I have never made much money from song-writing but I have won a few competitions and have had songs published; these successes have encouraged my belief that I have developed a degree of ability.

However, when I first started playing in a punk band in my teens, I could not sing and I struggled to learn how to play. I was always happy to thrash away on the bass guitar and let others be the creative force. I was too busy trying to look cool and tough. My friend in the band on the other hand was a naturally talented singer and songwriter who excelled as a musician from the first day he ever played and sang.

We worked hard and eventually, in the early 1980s, went on to win £10,000 and a major recording contract in a national BBC Battle of the Bands competition. A combination of greed, confusion, musical differences and copious amounts of Jazz Woodbines then caused us to split just as we were on the cusp of greatness. Such is life! However I believe that the influence of being around my naturally talented friend for a few years rubbed off on me as I eventually got into writing songs and have had a love for song-writing ever since. In spite of my best efforts I still sing like a foghorn but that is down to physiology. There are certain things for which you do need to have a degree of natural ability initially. There is a saying in the music business that states, "You can't polish a turd!"

> *"Thank goodness I was never sent to school; it would have rubbed off some of the originality."*
> Beatrix Potter

When looking to develop new ideas I suggest you begin your search by focusing on things that you like and enjoy. Think of your hobbies or things in your past that you have been good at or had a talent for. What areas do you have a lot of knowledge about? Do you have a favourite pastime or hobby that you particularly enjoy? Maybe you shone at something as a kid but have never had the chance to pursue it further.

When you use the following creativity script or self-hypnosis guide to connect with your creativity you will come up with some great ideas. Before you go into the trance state ask yourself to bring new ideas into your conscious thoughts, as all your truly great ideas lie deep inside your unconscious mind. This is where your true power and potential lie. My CD will help you here and you can also develop the following short self-hypnosis script for drawing upon your creativity.

I suggest you read the following script through a few times so that you learn it well before you practise it. Feel free to adapt it to suit your own aims.

Go into a quiet room where there are no distractions. Take a moment to get in a comfortable position, close your eyes and focus your attention on your breathing. Then begin breathing slowly and deeply – in through your nose and out through your mouth – in a circular breathing motion. Breathe away any tension left in your body with every slow out-breath, and allow yourself to relax more and more.

Continue this breathing pattern a dozen or more times and just clear away any unwanted thoughts so that your mind becomes still and quiet. Don't worry if you get the odd unwanted thought, just re-centre your mind and allow the thought to drift away again. Just focus on the stillness of the moment.

To guide yourself deeper into trance, silently and mentally count down from ten to one. Leave about five seconds between each number and feel every muscle in your body relax more and more. Maybe you can imagine yourself going down a beautiful staircase with each descending number. Feel yourself drifting down into deeper and deeper levels of mental and physical relaxation when you get to this point; almost as though you are weightless and just gently floating down through a dreamlike inner world – the inner world that leads to the genius inside you – the creative part of you.

At this point just allow yourself to totally relax and let go.

10... 9... Affirm to yourself: "I feel creative and inspired"... *8... 7...* "I believe in myself"... *6... 5...* "I have so much potential"... *4... 3...* "I live life with courage and confidence"... *2... 1....* Go deeper and deeper... to that powerful and resourceful part of you....

Now as you lie there in this stillness, feeling centred and very calm, connect with a part of you that is responsible for your creativity: the fun, creative part of you that is imaginative and carefree; the part that likes music and laughter. Take a moment to really feel this part of you and make a strong connection with it.

Now silently ask this creative part of you for guidance. Take a couple of minutes to do this. Ask this part for ideas for new ventures. Don't force it, just allow the ideas to come. Sometimes you will get ideas and inspiration later. The key is that you connect with this creative part now and open up that imaginative channel. When you do this you will find inspiration within you and you feel motivated to create and manifest new things in your life.

Take a five-minute gap here to be still and centred and to allow your creative ideas to come forward and develop.

After this point affirm to yourself that you will feel more creative and inspired in your daily life and that you can achieve many great things. State these affirmations as a reality now in the present tense. For example:

I find it easy to draw out my inner talents and express myself in many different ways.

I have an infinite source of creativity, which I draw upon to create many great things in my life.

I draw opportunities towards me and manifest many wonderful things in my life.

I take on new challenges with a fearless attitude.

I believe in myself and in my own ability.

When I make a positive decision I move decisively with complete self-belief.

I find it easy to remain focused and see things through as I have complete faith in myself now.

When you state these phrases, draw the words inside you and really believe they are a reality. Put your feelings into each phrase. You may want to add your own present tense phrases to call up creativity.

Then, when you are ready to finish, allow you mind to clear and count slowly upwards from one to ten, then open your eyes and come back to full waking consciousness: ... 1... 2... 3... 4... 5... 6... 7... 8... 9...10....

You will find new creative ideas will come to you now that you have opened up this channel. It may be that this will be made manifest when you get new ideas out of the blue a day or two later. Practise this exercise often when you are looking for ideas or inspiration.

Most creative geniuses have produced their greatest works when they were accessing their unconscious minds. Mozart could hear a long complex piece of music for the first time and then play it note for note in an instant. Paul McCartney woke up one morning with the song "Yesterday" in his head. The most frequently recorded song in the history of popular music!

Deciding to Set-Up a Business

Once you have some ideas for creating a product or service, research the market and if you feel that your idea has potential in the market place then *go for it*. Don't be put off if there is loads of competition as that also means there is a healthy market.

> *"The universe is full of magical things, patiently waiting for our wits to grow sharper."*
> Eden Phillpotts

When I produced my first hypnotherapy tapes I remember researching the market and finding there were many already out there but most were poorly produced and unimaginative in nature. This inspired me to produce tapes that were different and original. I put a lot of love and care into them, as I really wanted them to be effective and to help people. From the time I sold the first few home-made tapes to a local chemist chain in 1997, to the end of 2005, I sold over five million pounds-worth in retail value. When you get the product right and give people what they want, your product will sell itself.

If you decide to set up a business and pursue it with passion and real integrity you will be ahead of most of the competition anyway. Good quality and a positive intention are very important. If you are excited and proud of what you are selling, then customers will be drawn to your products. Creative marketing is also important and will propel your business ahead of most of the competition. I have added a short chapter at the end of this book about the practicalities of launching and marketing a new business (see p.113).

Thinking Big and Being Big-Hearted

When you formulate ideas for creating success, get into the habit of *thinking big*. Make your goals and plans big and bold and avoid getting bogged down in minutiae. If you make a few losses along the way, then put them down to experience and move on. Thinking big and being big-hearted will raise your energy and draw others towards you. I mentioned earlier that there is a universal law which states: "What you give out will come back to you". So, be open-hearted and generous in spirit as this is good for the soul.

Always combine a drive for success and abundance with an open heart. I have seen many cases where driven people become victims of money and success; but being abundant is not just about being rich and it won't solve all your problems. You can be financially abundant, but if your heart is closed you will be spiritually and emotionally bankrupt. Avoid becoming so exclusively focused on money that you forget how to enjoy life. Make time to smell the flowers on your journey. Encourage others to become a part of your success and involve people you care about in your plans. When you build a momentum and start to create success others will look to you for guidance and advice. So give out encouragement to others and be generous in spirit.

> "Without a rich heart, wealth is an ugly beggar."
> Ralph Waldo Emerson

A few years ago I was playing guitar in a covers duo in a restaurant where we had a residency. The venue had a number of rooms for various functions, and there were often many bands playing in the different rooms. One Saturday night there was a buzz around the place as the soul legend Geno Washington was playing in the main ballroom. Musicians would often pop their heads into other rooms to watch the other bands – then in typical *Spinal Tap* fashion get all bitchy about each other.

This particular evening Geno Washington walked into our room, and as he walked past us he smiled and said "you have a great sound". His words gave us a real lift from the drudgery of playing a four-hour set to largely uninterested diners. We were just a run-of-the-mill little covers duo there for people to have a jig to after their dinner. We had nothing more than a pleasant sound, but he told *us* we had a great sound! His simple gesture made us feel great and showed what a big-hearted person he obviously was.

Here is a short meditation that will help you to feel big-hearted. It can also help you develop more compassion for others.

Once again, I suggest you read the script through a few times so that you are familiar with the steps before you practise it.

Take a moment to get in a comfortable position, then close your eyes and focus on your breathing. Begin to breathe very slowly and deeply: in through your nose and out through your mouth. Make each breath long and deep, feel your rib cage expand as you breathe in. Continue this for a short while until all the tension disappears from your body, and you feel nice and relaxed.

Now imagine you are surrounded by a pure white light. See and feel this protective white light all around you, filling your aura. In this special place allow yourself to feel very secure and calm.

Become aware of your heart beating in your chest in a strong and steady rhythm, and imagine your heart is filled with pure white light. See the purity of the light in your heart and know that this special white light resonates with unconditional love. It may be the kind of love a mother feels for her baby. Take a moment to feel this white light of love growing bigger in your heart.

Now imagine the white light expanding out from your heart so that it begins to fill your whole body. As you do so, begin to connect with feelings of compassion and love for all things. Continue to imagine the white light expanding, filling your entire body and spreading out into your aura. Then imagine it expanding further still, as though this spark of light has grown so strong that it now projects out and away from you in every direction. Connect with this deep feeling of love and compassion growing stronger and stronger as the white light grows ever brighter, as it reaches further and further.

Now imagine your white light of unconditional love reaching out and engulfing others: maybe people you know or people you want to reach. Experience a strong feeling of love for these people and feel deep compassion for their struggles and troubles. See their faults and weaknesses as manifestations of difficulties in their life.

As you continue to imagine the white light illuminating everything before you and expanding ever further, connect now with a feeling of love and compassion and knowledge and personal power.

Just stay in this moment for a short time so you can continue to reach out with your unconditional love. Then when you are ready count from one to three: *1...* *2...* *3....* Open your eyes and come back to full waking consciousness.

You can adapt this visualization as preparation for making a good impression in specific meetings.

Giving and Receiving

Giving and receiving should be done in equal measure so you create a free-flowing energy. I know someone who made a promise to donate 10 per cent of any money she ever won to charity. She won the first prize in a lottery and, true to her word, gave 10 per cent to her favourite charity. When you have that kind of attitude towards money, it liberates you and enables you to enjoy your affluence much more. There is a subtle freedom that comes from being able to give so easily. This in turn will help you to receive more easily.

Most people say they want to have more money but oddly enough will reject abundance by saying no, when it is offered. Have you ever said no to someone who has offered you money? Have you ever rejected financial help when it has been offered because it made you feel awkward? That is a hang-up and something you need to overcome urgently if it applies to you. How can you ever create free-flowing

abundance if you reject it when it is freely offered to you? People sometimes do this because they want to be seen to be nice or honourable or because of a misplaced social grace. That is appropriate at certain times but if you do it too often, you are blocking your own abundance. Don't be afraid to take money when it is offered to you, especially if you have earned it. Step up, collect, and be thankful. As long as you are being generous yourself then you create a healthy flow.

The only exception to the rule is where someone is giving you something and then expects something in return; this is an instance where money can be used in the wrong way. There are those who may pretend they are doing you a favour or helping you out but if they covertly want something back, then it is not help at all. So avoid any such trap. If you feel this happening then you would be quite right to reject what is offered. Always give and receive freely without condition.

The next time someone is generous to you, say to yourself, "I deserve it and accept the offer of help with a positive feeling." If you can't do this you will need to work on this attitude as it an important area to master on your journey to abundance. Use one of the self-hypnosis or meditation techniques to practise accepting money freely and easily. If you feel the need, practise specific affirmations on giving and receiving like these:

I find it easy to accept other people's generosity.

I give and receive easily.

I treat people honourably.

I accept that money comes to me easily now.

I am generous and abundant.

I deserve to be wealthy.

Summary

▶▶ **Be open to all possibilities of becoming wealthy.**

▶▶ **Use your creativity to find a lucrative new venture that can make you money.**

▶▶ **Create ideas for starting a new business or sideline with big potential.**

▶▶ **Think big and be big-hearted and generous in spirit.**

▶▶ **Learn to give and receive freely and naturally.**

Step 6 – Using Your Intuition

Connecting with Your Deep Inner feelings

Once you have decided upon your goals and aims, you will need to take time to visualise everything happening as you want it to. Imagine yourself meeting the right people, being in the right place at the right time, and always getting what you need. Once you get in the habit of visualising, and using your inner resources, you will also become much more intuitive, and will find that you make many more right decisions than wrong ones. The whole process of creating abundance becomes holistic when you are using your potential to the full. After a while you begin to trust your judgement and intuition completely; so much so that you will always expect things to reach a positive conclusion.

> "All children are artists. The problem is how to remain an artist once they grow up."
> Pablo Picasso

If ever you have a dilemma and you are not sure which decision to make, use the following visualisation technique.

Please read this script through a few times so that you learn it well before you practise it. Feel free to adapt it to suit your own aims. Always take your time when reading the self-hypnosis scripts and allow yourself to go as deep into trance as you can.

Go to a quiet room where there are no distractions and take a moment to get in a comfortable position. Close your eyes and focus your attention on your breathing; then begin breathing slowly and deeply – in through your nose and out through your mouth – in a circular breathing motion. With every slow out-breath, breathe away any tension left in your body, and feel yourself relax more and more. Continue this breathing pattern a dozen or more times or for as long as you feel comfortable, then gradually let your breathing return to normal.

You need to let your mind become very still and quiet and allow any unwanted thoughts to drift away. A good way to do this is to imagine for a moment that you are looking up at the sky on a pleasant summer's day. You notice a few small clouds floating in the blue sky. You watch as the clouds drift across the sky and then fade away. After a while the sky becomes clear and as it does so your mind will also become clear and calm. As you see the sky become clear so your mind becomes very still and quiet.

Now with your mind still and quiet, and your body relaxed and calm, take a few deep breaths and connect with the stillness inside you. Tune in to your intuition, your subtle inner feelings. Take a moment to enjoy the connection to your inner feelings. Take all the time you need here.

Then silently ask the question to which you need an answer or guidance.

Which direction should I take?
Or
Which direction is the best one for me?

Then still your mind again and be guided by your feelings. It is important that you are guided by your feelings and not your thoughts. Make the distinction here. What is your deep inner feeling saying to you? Which way is it directing you? Notice which direction feels like the right one.

With practice, and in your centred space, your inner feelings will guide you in the right direction. If nothing comes to you straight away just centre yourself again and ask the question once more. Stay in that peaceful state for as long as it takes. You have all the time you need and there is no better place to be. This is the place where you truly empower yourself.

If no clear direction or guidance comes, then state that you will be guided to the solution when the time is right.

If you have the answer you need, affirm that this powerful connection to your intuition will stay with you and guide you continually in your everyday life. State in the present tense:

I make good decisions and wise choices.

I have so much knowledge and wisdom inside me.

I draw upon my knowledge and achieve many great things.

I always find it easy to raise my consciousness and connect with the infinite creativity inside me.

I feel empowered and guided by my inner wisdom.

Add your own affirmations here.

Then, when you are ready, slowly count upwards from one to ten and open your eyes to come back to full waking consciousness... *1... 2... 3... 4... 5... 6... 7... 8... 9... 10....*

If you don't immediately have a clear idea of the best way forward, it will come to you very soon.

Trusting Your Instincts

A few years ago, when my business began to take off, I decided to buy a larger house. I could also just about stretch to keeping my existing house, which I had decided I would rent out as an investment. As there had been a housing boom for a few years there was a lot of speculation about where the market was going. A part of me was a little apprehensive about taking on two big mortgages. However my gut feeling was telling me to go for it. Then one day, nearing the time that I was to sign the legal papers for both mortgages, I bought a national daily paper and the front-page headline screamed, "HOUSE PRICES SURE TO PLUMMET". The article quoted so-called leading economic experts who went into depth about why the housing market could not sustain itself for a minute longer and house prices were about to collapse. This powerful headline gave me the willies and so I changed track and pulled out of the deal to keep my existing property. This proved to be a big mistake as house prices continued to rocket. Within two years of selling the house, it had more than doubled in value. Buying the newspaper on that day had in effect cost me £100,000.

The episode taught me two lessons: to stick by my gut feelings and never to buy newspapers. I genuinely do not buy newspapers anymore as they are often full of hysterical fear and have their own agendas in reporting news. The experience didn't make me bitter, although I was a bit miffed for a while that I had been swayed away from my original decision which had proved to be spot on; but it did teach me to trust my own instincts and judgement a lot more and to resolve to let that guide me in future.

> "I never get the accountants in before I start a business. It's done on gut feeling."
> Richard Branson

More recently, when I wanted to buy a property abroad as an investment, a few well-meaning friends told me that my choice of area was wrong because the market there had always been sluggish. This time I ignored any external advice and followed through trusting my gut feeling. I bought a property that was due to be built on a new development in an up-and-coming area. It takes a leap of faith to buy an overseas property that doesn't yet exist – except as a sandpit that a developer assures you will soon become your new luxury home! The house took nine months to build and in that time the area went through an unprecedented boom. By the time the house was built it had appreciated by 50 per cent in value. In a nutshell I was in exactly the right place at exactly the right time – but then I had been meditating on that affirmation for a long time beforehand.

Our own intuition will guide us better than any external advice as we know instinctively what is best for ourselves. We have had this ability since the beginning of time. In prehistoric times when we were more tuned into nature, our sixth sense could alert us to danger. This intuitive sense is also prevalent in animals that don't have the intellectual consciousness that inhibits this subtle form of communication. It was widely reported that very few animals perished in the Asian Tsunami disaster of Christmas 2004 as the animals sensed it was coming and fled to higher ground before the waves hit.

When you learn to trust and connect with your intuitive feelings, you will make many more good decisions than bad ones. There may also be times when you will need to pull back and re-evaluate things and you will need to be intuitively aware of this; even the most successful plans will have ups and downs on the way. You will need to be flexible and adaptive and use your subtle feelings to make shrewd decisions.

Eventually, when you get into a flow where things happen easily and fall into place, many more doors will open for you, but it doesn't always happen straight away. Initially things may be slow but once the momentum builds it can be unstoppable.

The momentum is related to the energy that you put into your goals, and if you energise your plan it will succeed. It then comes down to how much you want and how far you want to go. There are people walking this earth who started life with nothing but who became billionaires because of their ability to focus their energy. Imagine creating assets worth one thousand million pounds (or dollars). We live in an age where it is possible to achieve such things.

Summary

▶▶ Learn how to connect with your intuition.

▶▶ Use visualisation techniques to connect and develop your intuition for guidance.

▶▶ Trust your instincts to guide you to make good decisions.

Step 7 – Creating a Powerful and Lasting Desire to Become Successful

Building Your Motivation to Succeed

My best mate from childhood was a good lad called Terry who became a self-made millionaire in his early twenties. By the time he reached his thirties he was making so much money he was appearing on the UK rich-list of top earners. Following our teens we had taken different paths in life. My ego was pulling me in the hedonistic direction of the pop world and his focus was on achieving financial success. We lost touch for a few years but met up in our mid-twenties when we discovered we were living near each other in south London.

Terry was living in a luxury penthouse apartment in an upmarket area while three miles away I was living at the top of a council tower block in a rough area. We went out a few times but it was difficult to re-connect as our circumstances were so different. I would joke that we had both rocketed with similar speed to opposite ends of the social scale, but that didn't hide the fact that I felt I was a complete failure. This was highlighted even more so by my friend's success. I've always felt it would make a great story for a film: two boyhood best friends lose touch and then meet up again, only to find that one is a millionaire and the other has lost his way and is broke and struggling.

I believed then and I believe now that you make your own success in life. I remember saying this even at that time, when I had nothing. The experience of meeting my friend again made me refocus on my life and become a little bit more determined to succeed. Fear of failure became a powerful motivator and that period was a positive turning point as I figured that as kids we had been equals: both reasonably smart but nothing outstanding. What were the factors that had taken our lives in such different directions? After some self-analysis I realised that where my friend was disciplined I was lazy, where he was determined I had been half-hearted and where he had belief I had none.

I decided to change things and raise my game. I didn't know how or where to begin but I did start to become very determined to make something of myself. Had I read books like this one and learnt the power of self-hypnosis at that time, I might have created my success much more quickly. However, through trial and error I eventually pulled myself out of my slumber.

> *"To accomplish great things, we must not only act, but also dream, not only plan, but also believe."*
> Anatole France

You need to get motivated and be hungry for success and remain focused. What is it that is motivating you? *Why* do you want to be successful?

It is good to ask yourself these questions so you are clear about what you want and why you want it. How badly do you want to be successful? What is going to keep you motivated if times get tough?

My motivation was the fear of failure and the desire to prove I wasn't the waster I had so often been labelled in my childhood. Find your motivation and get yourself fired up. Always remember: the only way you can fail is if you quit!

Being Single-Minded and Self-Disciplined

When I eventually got the fire in my belly, I started with the basics, by getting rid of anything that was holding me back. I began to get healthy in my mind and body. I quit smoking, cut out alcohol, started swimming regularly and eating more healthily. I also started to read more, especially self-help titles and books that would inspire and educate me, as I didn't get much of an education at school. I also began hanging out with more positive people and gently moved away from anyone who was a bit of an energy drain.

This stage can be difficult at times, because when you make a shift like this you can distance yourself from people you have been close to – even family members. It can be a lonely road at times. When you start to make changes in yourself, even though they are positive changes, you may find your relationships change. This can be tough and testing. It happens because people around you can feel insecure when you change, as they may fear losing you; or, as in the case of my successful friend Terry and myself, when a person moves onward and upward it can make others feel insecure and highlight their own failings.

You have to move on regardless, because being successful is more important than keeping your friends happy. I don't mean plough on in a ruthless, "don't give a toss" way; just don't get pulled back down because of other people's insecurities. Those who really care about you will eventually come around if they see that what you are doing is for the right reasons. You will win their respect in the end.

> "Keep away from people who try to belittle your ambitions. Small people always do that, but the really great make you feel that you, too, can become great."
> Mark Twain

There is a metaphor that I love that explains this weird quirk of human behaviour:

A man goes into a restaurant where he notices a large bucket full of live crabs. He notices that one crab is climbing up the bucket wall and it looks like he is going to escape. So the man informs the waiter. The waiter tells the man that the crab will never escape as every time one of them gets near to the top, the other crabs in the bucket will always pull it back.

You may well encounter these little obstacles on your journey to abundance, but if you are single-minded and courageous you will rise above any such challenges and tests. Try to do this by avoiding conflict or getting embroiled in debate about why you are making changes. Just continue on your journey in a disciplined and modest way. Remember to keep your ego in check at all times as this is about self-empowerment not about impressing others. Make your plans big and bold but avoid talking about them unless it is necessary as too much idle chatter can dissipate your energy. Even when things start to happen, avoid talking too much about your success, as it is easy to make others feel insecure especially if they are struggling. Your success will inspire people around you without you needing to say anything about it.

Being Flexible

Once your plans are made and all the key ingredients are in place, you need to take action. However, you may need to make many alterations to your plans. That is fine, as you will need to be flexible and able to adapt quickly as you spot new opportunities in the marketplace. In this modern day and age there is little security: large companies go bust overnight and hard-accumulated pensions can devalue rapidly in a few years. Change is the only certainty in life and you will need to apply an understanding of this to your business: be adaptable and embrace change.

Even when you hit the abundant "flow" state, you will still need to keep moving forward with new ideas so that your vision stays fresh and vibrant. However, once things start to fly and the money rolls in, you will need to work even harder as it will go against the grain to turn away good opportunities when you have wanted them so badly in the past. The best thing about success is that it opens many new doors and, after your initial effort in getting the business up and running on a shoestring, the whole thing should start to flow much more easily. So be aware and quick on your feet and when opportunity beckons grasp it with both hands.

Here is a script to take you into a deeper state of self-hypnosis that will help you to stay focused, maintain motivation and build self-belief. The affirmations will help you if you ever experience any self-doubt on your journey.

As always read this script through a few times so that you are familiar with the steps before you practise it.

Take a moment to get in a comfortable position, close your eyes and focus on your breathing. Begin to breathe very slowly and deeply – in through your nose and out through your mouth. Make each breath long and deep, feel your rib cage expand as you breathe in. Continue this for a short while until all the tension disappears from your body, and you feel nice and relaxed.

Continue to breathe slowly and deeply in a steady, rhythmical breathing pattern and when you reach the top of your breath hold it for three seconds: ... *1... 2... 3....* Then silently and mentally count to five on every out-breath: ... *1... 2... 3... 4... 5...* Relax more and more with every slow out-breath.

Any time you have a stressful situation remember this simple breathing exercise as it will help you to get into a state where you feel calm and in control of your thoughts and feelings.

Now I want you to practise a more instant way of going into trance. Slowly and steadily count from one to three either silently or out loud: ...*1... 2... 3....* When you reach the number three you will become ten times more deeply relaxed. You will be ten times deeper inside that powerful part of your self where your true potential lies: your creativity, your courage, and your self-belief. So, at the very point you reach the number three, you go deep down into a very relaxed state. So, ready? ... *1... 2... 3....* Go there now. Deeper relaxed than you've been in a long time. Every cell in your mind, body and spirit resonates with positive energy now. Take a short while to enjoy these wonderful positive feelings.

PAUSE

Now if you don't master this first time do not worry as it may take practice before you can go into a deep trance very quickly. If this doesn't work for you, you can always use one of the previous trance-deepening methods.

Once you get into that deeply relaxed and centred space I want you to repeat as many of the following affirmations as you wish. Say them with real feeling and emotion. Imagine every part of you repeating the affirmations with complete conviction and self-belief, in the present tense. Draw the phrases deep inside you when you say them:

Select a few of these affirmation phrases that most suit your needs and aims.

I believe in myself.

I draw opportunities towards me.

I move away from struggle and conflict and into a flow state.

I feel dynamic and full of ideas and enthusiasm.

I live my life to the full with courage and self-belief.

I go beyond old limitations and draw out my true potential.

I deserve to be abundant and prosperous.

I continue to create many more opportunities in my life.

I think and feel more positively all the time.

I attract other positive people towards me.

The affirmations above are examples. Feel free to adapt them for your specific goals.

Once you have stated and focused on your affirmations you can compound these new beliefs by the counting method. Once again count from one to three. This time, when you reach the number three, affirm that these positive new beliefs will sink ten times deeper into your unconscious mind, and the positive feelings will grow ten times stronger. Ten times deeper inside to that powerful part of your self where your true potential lies. So, ready? Slowly count to three: *1... 2... 3...* and feel yourself drawing all your new beliefs deeply into your inner consciousness. Every cell in your mind, body and spirit is resonating with positive energy now. Take a moment to enjoy this feeling and to accept every new belief as a reality.

When you are ready, slowly count from one to ten, open your eyes and come back to full waking consciousness.

Remaining Strong and Centred

You need to keep your energy level high and stay positive and focused to stay on course. Never hanker or yearn after things, as this will only push them away from you. The law of attraction states that we attract into our lives the things we believe we deserve at a deep level. It is like an unseen force and is very powerful, so you must work on your deep inner feelings and stay positive.

If you want something in life or require something from someone, visualise and affirm it coming to you. This is the way you empower yourself: by being strong and centred and accepting that abundance is natural and comes to you easily. It is such an attractive quality that when you master it, people will be drawn towards you and be keen to help you. If you are needy and wanting, people will bypass you, as your weakness will make them feel insecure. Even when you are hoping to clinch a crucial deal, adopt an attitude where you accept that if it is meant to happen it will happen; if it is not meant to be, then it won't happen.

It is unlikely that you will clinch every deal you go after even with the most positive of mindsets. However, with a relaxed attitude where you are strong, centred and together, you will always give yourself the best possible opportunity. In the words of the song: "You can't always get what you want... but if you try real hard you might just get what you need." Mick Jagger – what a sage!

Building Your Energy

Life is not unfair and there is no bad luck when you get into the flow state and create positive energy all around you. You will begin to meet the right people at the right time, be in the right place at the right time because that is what you are projecting out from deep within you. The universe will deliver to you exactly what you are giving out. I am no expert on metaphysics but I do believe that you can create powerful energy inside you that will deliver to you absolutely anything you want. If you think about it, everything in the known universe is made up of atoms and molecules that vibrate together to create energy. The chair or bed you are sitting or lying on now is made up of atoms and molecules that vibrate so fast that they create a solid mass. Energy work is important, because when you raise your energy through your positive inner work you will increase your vibrational energy. You will then find you attract more opportunities towards you and life starts to flow more easily

> *"The harder I work, the luckier I get."*
> Samuel Goldwyn

Summary

▶▶ **Focus on things that motivate you. Build your energy and a continuous burning desire to succeed.**

▶▶ **Don't let anyone or anything hold you back. Become single-minded in your pursuit of success.**

▶▶ **Learn the motivation and belief self-hypnosis script.**

Step 8 – Overcoming Setbacks and Staying Focused on Success

Maintaining the Momentum

One of the main reasons people fail to succeed is that they start out very motivated and fired up, but after a few knockbacks lose that initial enthusiasm. You can't expect to go through this whole journey charged with positivity every second of the day like a demented game show host.

Everything in life goes in cycles and you are going to experience ups and downs. Along with the successes will be the occasional setback. This is where you require guile, resilience and a need to stay on track. If things are not flowing as you would like, these are the times to pull back and re-evaluate. Give more attention to your inner work: keep affirming and visualising and asking for guidance. If something isn't working, don't charge on in a bullish fashion, as this can lead to burnout.

> "The world makes way for the person who knows where he is going."
> Ralph Waldo Emerson

Look inside yourself and connect with your inner creativity and intuition. Perhaps a slight adjustment is all that is needed. If you learn to connect with your feelings, rather than trying to intellectualise everything, you will always find solutions. If you are faced with a dilemma or you are stuck in some way, quieten your mind and notice the feelings you have about the situation. Remember that inside each one of us is an unlimited source of creativity and wisdom. To get to it you need to learn to bypass your intellect.

Connecting with Your Higher Self

It can help at times to give problems up to your higher power or whatever force you believe is guiding or helping you through life. So when you have a problem always create time to switch off, and go inside your self and ask for guidance. Affirm that the solution will come to you when you need it. Maybe it is that you are asking your own deep inner self for solutions; or those of you with more spiritual beliefs may ask your guides and angels for help.

I once had an experience which changed my beliefs and made me realise that there is help out there in many forms. I was facing a dilemma in my career and had a problem with a particular business associate and was unsure which way to turn. Around this time someone told me in passing of a medium who was giving a talk at a venue nearby in the next few days. I had heard that this lady was very good but that she rarely made public appearances, so I thought this might be an opportunity to get some guidance and insight.

On the journey to the meeting I was projecting the thought that I needed help, and I was asking for guidance for my particular dilemma. When I arrived at the small gathering I was disappointed to find that the medium was not giving individual readings and was talking to the group only about mediumship and spirituality in

> *"For those that believe, no explanation is necessary. For those that do not, no explanation will suffice."*
> Anon

general. However, at the end of her talk an amazing thing happened. She made a beeline for me and said that although she hadn't planned to do any readings she had received some messages that she felt she had to relay to me. She went on to give me answers to all the questions that I had been projecting, even to the point of correctly naming the business associate with whom I had the dilemma. I had never met this medium in my life before and the way in which she gave me the messages left me totally gobsmacked. On the journey home I felt so uplifted that the universe had delivered to me these answers with such clarity.

There is a saying that goes: "For those that believe, no explanation is necessary. For those that do not, no explanation will suffice." After many positive experiences like the one just described, I tend to fall into the former category, but I have friends and family who fall into the latter. Whenever we debate the age-old belief conundrum I argue that you do actually have to ask for help in the first place by projecting your problem out there. Then be aware of the guidance and help that comes to you. The solutions don't always arrive as clearly as mine did on this particular occasion. More often than not, they are very subtle, but my belief is that when you are awake and aware and on your vocational path and fulfilling your true potential, you will receive unlimited guidance and help.

Try to avoid getting so embroiled in the day-to-day mechanics of a situation that you fail to spot the solutions to a problem. Remember the old maxim "Sometimes you can't see the wood for the trees". This can often occur in business where you have many things going on at the same time. Always make time to step back and evaluate the bigger picture, and be open to all possibilities.

Here is a short script for connecting with your higher self.

Don't worry if this script doesn't feel right for you or seems a bit wacky. It is not for everyone so feel free to skip it if you wish or adapt it to suit your beliefs. Read the script through a few times so that you are familiar with the steps before you practise it.

Take a moment to get in a comfortable position, close your eyes and focus on your breathing. Once again begin to breathe deeply and slowly, in a steady rhythmical breathing pattern. Breathe in through your nose and out through your mouth creating a circular breathing motion. At the top of your breath hold it for three seconds: *1... 2... 3...* then silently and mentally count to five on every out-breath: *1... 2... 3... 4... 5....* As you breathe out, let go of any tension left in your body.

Now as you lie there relaxing more and more, imagine you are gazing up into the night sky. You notice many bright and beautiful stars lighting up the heavens. As you marvel at this wonderful picture you notice one particular star shining brightly, more so than all the others: a shimmering glowing star, shining so brightly in the night sky, radiating energy and light. Your whole attention is drawn to this star. You feel there is something special about it, as though it is there to help you in some way. You sense that this star holds the key to everything you need to know to help you to go forward successfully in life. This star will guide you and bring you knowledge.

You become completely focused on the tiny, white ball of light and notice it coming nearer to you but still remaining the size of a tiny ball. See it come closer and closer until it is hovering just above the crown of your head. Just floating in mid-air above the top of your head. You may at this point feel a slight tingling sensation or a warm, comforting glow.

Now you feel that a part of you is in this special light... the spirit part of you that knows your life journey and vocation... the infinite wisdom part of you that is your higher self. Now draw this ball of light inside you so that you are filled with understanding and knowledge.

Affirm to yourself:

I am open to higher levels of knowledge.

I have great wisdom and understanding.

I am aware and enlightened.

I understand my journey in life.

My vocation becomes clear.

Then, when you are ready, slowly count from one to ten, and open your eyes and come back to full waking consciousness.

Live in the Here and Now

Never yearn for things you don't have and avoid living in the future. People often live for tomorrow and long for the day their mortgage will be paid off or their pension matures. They presume life is going to come good when they get to this point in their lives. Living for tomorrow is a bad habit as it disempowers you and creates a belief that the good times are always ahead of you. Keep your focus on the here and now: when you visualise your abundant lifestyle, see it as though it is in the present. Imagine you are driving the Bentley or the Aston Martin right now!

It is liberating to free yourself from wanting and being needy in all areas of your life. Work on being more self-contained and try not to rely on others for your wellbeing and happiness. You will become much stronger in this way and you will build your inner strength. This in turn begins to attract things towards you. Work on your self and nurture the good in you. Be disciplined and focused while keeping your mind open and free.

Martial arts, yoga and T'ai Chi are great for developing this type of discipline. If you are starting a new business venture you might consider taking up one of these disciplines at the same time. This would help give balance between your drive to succeed in business and your mental and emotional wellbeing. It would also help you to keep your energy levels up and to develop a more holistic approach to creating abundance in your life.

Work on keeping your emotions in check and go with the ebb and flow of life. Don't get too carried away when you reach highs or too down if you hit low-points or setbacks. If you have a few failures or make mistakes on your journey to abundance, avoid getting over-emotional. Just accept you have learnt a lesson and you won't make that error again.

Step out of Your Comfort Zone

To achieve success you will also need to move beyond your personal comfort zone and take a few chances. Some of the most successful people in the world are also huge risk takers. An example once again is Richard Branson – a man with a very healthy billion pound portfolio that would prompt most people to live in five-star luxury and mollycoddled comfort until the end of their days. Not Richard, who is so driven he gambled everything on an extremely high-risk ballooning challenge in pursuit of a world record. Admirable stuff. His attitude provides an insight into why he became a billionaire within a relatively short space of time. I've always admired people who are bold risk takers. I can't see much point in standing still and clinging to perceived security and safety just because it is familiar. Moving forward and creating success will bring you more security anyway, but ironically you have to take risks to get it.

> *"Don't be afraid of making mistakes on this journey, as mistakes are learning curves. Don't see them as failures."*
> Anon

Using role models

It can sometimes help to focus on other successful people whose achievements you aspire to. Think of someone who is a high achiever and who has qualities that you admire. Use their success as an inspiration and accept that you can do the same. There follows an NLP* modelling technique which will help you learn to absorb and assimilate the same qualities that someone who inspires you possesses. Think as though you are studying the ways and methods that help them to succeed and then import these winning characteristics into your consciousness.

---

* NLP stands for Neuro-Linguistic Programming. NLP is a therapeutic model for effective communicating, goal setting, influencing, accelerated learning and modifying behaviour.

Take a moment to get comfortable and close your eyes. Breathe very slowly and deeply in through your nose and out through your mouth. Make each breath long and deep and relax more and more with every slow out-breath.

Now I want you to focus on someone whose success inspires you. It can be a person you know, or even a famous sportsman, or maybe a celebrity whom you admire. Think of someone who's achieved something that you aspire to.

Take a moment to see this person in your mind's eye, and focus on their achievements. Just focus on their qualities and things that you like about them. Take a moment to focus on these.

PAUSE

Now imagine that all of these qualities are becoming part of you. Feel as though you are drawing these skills deep inside yourself. Whatever it is that you like about them, imagine you are absorbing and assimilating this talent now. Now accept that you express yourself in a similar way with the same great ability. Imagine these skills are a part of you now.

Now visualise yourself expressing these positive traits with the same confidence, self-belief and determination as the person you admire. Use these skills to help you achieve your goals and ambitions. Take a moment to focus on this. Be creative and use all of your senses when you visualise yourself expressing these new characteristics that will help you achieve great success.

PAUSE

Then when you are ready to finish, allow your mind to clear and slowly count from one to three and open your eyes and come back to full waking consciousness.

You can adapt this NLP technique for many different aims. For example, if your goal is to become a successful sportsman, model your game on the very top performers in your chosen sport. If you want to set the financial world alight, model yourself on a person whom you admire as having great success in this area. If you want to be a successful musician, draw upon and focus on the positive traits of a famous musician whose work inspires you.

Be creative when you use these techniques and adapt them for your specific goals. And then practise them regularly!

Don't Buy Into Fear

Try to avoid negative energy, especially from all-pervasive media bombardment. I am not saying sell your TV, but be selective about what you fill your thoughts with. It is about getting a balance. Be aware of just how TV and radio can influence your thinking on an unconscious level. Even if the radio is being played in another room, or you can't hear it clearly, your unconscious will still absorb much of the output – and, believe me, media advertisers know how to manipulate you. The psychological illusionist Derren Brown has often demonstrated in his TV shows the level to which we can be manipulated by the media. If you cut out some of the media intrusion, you will have more time for your own thoughts, so be selective about what you watch and listen.

> "Many a small thing has been made large by the right kind of advertising."
> Mark Twain

Many people are terrified of flying these days even though it is a very safe form of travel. When a plane crash occurs it is all over the media in graphic detail, which often terrifies people. In reality it should not, as statistically you have more chance of being in a car crash, but most people have no fear of travelling by car. I have close family members who refuse to fly point blank, but they are the ones who will avidly watch plane crash documentaries!

Always remember that you have unlimited power and potential inside you, and you need to release any conditioning that has disempowered you. It is not always easy to do, as we are not taught how to be self-empowered. Nor have we ever been. Throughout the centuries religious orders controlled the masses through fear; people were sold the lie that their power lay outside them in the form of a holy deity, and that failure to worship this or that god would render their life worthless. It still goes on today, but people are smarter now and many are reclaiming their power. The free-spirited and open-minded are becoming empowered once again and many are realising that they don't need a load of man-made dogma to connect with their god or higher power.

When you pursue your goals be bold and courageous and never let fear hold you back. You will not make perfect decisions every time, but learn from any errors and move onward and upwards with courage and self-belief. Life itself is a gamble and there is not

> "There is no security in life, only opportunity."
> Mark Twain

much security in the world these days. However, if you invest in something that is solid and real and in which you believe, you will be successful. How successful you become depends on the energy you invest in your self and in your vision.

Summary

▶▶ Learn to overcome setbacks and remain resilient. "You only fail if you quit" should be your mantra.

▶▶ Use every resource and ask for guidance from your higher power depending on your beliefs.

▶▶ Avoid living for tomorrow. Live in the present moment.

▶▶ Detach yourself from media scare stories and fearmongers.

Final Thoughts

Enjoy your Journey to Abundance

Enjoy your journey, develop the art of being positive, and make creating opportunities a way of life. What can be better than that? How fulfilling is spending night after night sitting on a sofa watching TV? Watching crap that fills the masses with fear, or soap operas that dull the brain cells? It is easy to do and entertaining but how rewarding is it?

You have unlimited potential at your disposal and you can use your creativity and inner talents to create a new lifestyle if you become diligent and focused for a sustained period of time. At the end of the day being successful will be one of the most rewarding and satisfying things you can do with your life.

I always used to fear that when I was old I would feel as if I had not achieved much. This fear motivated me, in a big way, to get myself into gear and create positive things in my life. It is not such a big fear now. For a troubled kid who was expelled from school at 15 I feel I have proved a few teachers wrong! In the end I turned a negative situation into a positive one. I used the negative impact of constantly being told that I was useless and a failure to motivate me to succeed. Whatever it is that drives you, use it to the full. Turn any negative experiences into positive ones. Sometimes this is easier said than done I know, but if you work at it and use your inner resources you can overcome any obstacles.

Finally

I spent many years wishing I could become successful and wealthy and hoping for good fortune. I now realise that much of that yearning and hoping was a waste of time and energy. When I learnt many of the principles and techniques laid out in this book I became armed with knowledge. When I then put the principles into action and became focused and disciplined I changed my circumstances very quickly, and success came easily to me, in many different ways.

Absolutely anything you want is out there, just waiting for you to simply step up and collect it. So let go of your fears, live your life with courage and confidence, and shoot for the moon. Your dreams will come true every time. All you have to do is build enough energy and stay focused.

So, I wish you well and hope that you take everything from this book that you need to create success in your life.

All the very best

Glenn Harrold

Summary: Sequence to Abundance

1. If you are struggling financially cut back on any excesses and live minimally for a time if need be; then you can start to breathe and focus on abundance.

2. Let go of any negativity surrounding your thoughts about money and reprogramme yourself to accept that money is easy to come by and that it is your divine right to become successful and wealthy.

3. List your goals and affirmations in detail and recite them as often as possible. Use self-hypnosis and visualisation to compound them at a deep level.

4. Learn how to use hypnotherapy to compound your goals and affirmations and use self-hypnosis to empower yourself.

5. Take practical steps towards your goals and get yourself fired up as everything you want is waiting for you to step up and collect it.

6. Develop your intuition to help guide you in the right direction. Learn to connect with your deep inner feelings and trust your instincts.

7. Create a powerful desire to succeed and be single-minded in pursuit of your goals.

8. Stay diligent, overcome setbacks and maintain momentum. Be resolute and always reaffirm your goals and affirmations.

Final thoughts – Make the journey to abundance a part of your life. Enjoy the ride and never become obsessed by possessions and money – it is only paper after all.

Appendices

How the CD Works

How to use the CD

The CD is completely safe, very effective, and comes with a clear set of instructions. There are two tracks on the CD. The first track is a full 30-minute hypnotherapy session, which you can use repeatedly. The second track is a shorter version, which can be used as a booster session anytime that you don't have time for track one. For more info on this please visit the "frequently asked questions" page on our website –

www.hypnosisaudio.com

You must on no account listen to the CD while driving a vehicle or using heavy machinery. Both recordings on this CD will guide you into a state of complete physical and mental relaxation, so it is recommended that you listen while you are lying down in a place where you won't be disturbed. For maximum effect we strongly recommend that you listen through headphones.

Don't worry if you fall asleep before you reach the end of either track, as your unconscious mind is very capable of absorbing all the positive suggestions even during light sleep states.

Hypnotherapy content, affirmations and sound effects on the CD

The first thing you will hear is the introductory music and an explanation of how the CD works. After a few minutes the music fades and you are left with a pleasant voice and some uniquely created sound effects, which will guide you into a state of complete physical and mental relaxation. The special sound effects have been recorded at 60 b.p.m, to help synchronise the left and right hemispheres of the brain and create a very receptive learning state.

The recording includes echoed affirmations that pan slowly from left to right in your speakers or headphones. This deeply relaxing and unique effect is very hypnotic and helps you to absorb each affirmation deeply. In this receptive and relaxed state you will also be given a number of positive post-hypnotic suggestions to help you achieve your abundance goals.

At the end of the recording you will be brought back gently to full waking consciousness with a combination of suggestions and music. There are also a number of positive subliminal messages embedded in the fade-out music, which facilitate the overall effect.

The affirmations and subliminal suggestions on the CD are as follows:

I release any negative feeling towards money and success.

I am always in the right place at the right time.

Abundance flows freely and naturally to me.

All of my needs are constantly met.

I deserve to be wealthy and successful.

I feel very comfortable making lots of money.

I accept unconditional abundance on every level.

As outlined in my guide to hypnosis on p.43, there are five stages typical of a clinical hypnotherapy session:

1. **The introduction**

2. **The induction**

3. **The trance deepening**

4. **Post-hypnotic suggestions and affirmations**

5. **The awakening**

The important thing to remember is that although you are being guided, you will always remain in full control of the whole process. If at any time you need to awaken, you just open your eyes and you will be wide awake.

How long should I use the CD for?

There are no hard and fast rules as to how long the CD should be used, but here are some guidelines.

The hypnosis CD will work differently for each individual. It is impossible to give an estimated time for use, but after listening a few times you should begin to notice some positive changes in your attitude to creating success. Sometimes the positive changes will be instant and dramatic, or you may experience a gradual, subtle progression into a new pattern of behaviour over time.

You can listen to the CD as often as you like. The key to absorbing hypnotic suggestion is compounding. This means that the more you hear the suggestions, the quicker your unconscious mind will get the message. You then respond to the suggestions automatically in your everyday life.

For maximum effect listen to the CD on a daily basis until you have reached your goal or overcome a problem. You may choose to continue listening even after you reach your goal, as it will always help to reinforce everything you have learned and keep you focused.

The best way to self-hypnotise or absorb the Abundance CD content is to believe implicitly that all the suggestions are real. Draw the suggestions inside your mind while you are deeply relaxed. Your unconscious mind doesn't distinguish between what is real and imagined. The more you imagine and visualise the more you override old beliefs and install positive new ones. Don't worry if you drift away or get distracted, just bring your mind back on track. Once these beliefs are absorbed into your unconscious, you will respond accordingly and begin to manifest everything you have programmed yourself to believe.

If you fall asleep listening to the CD but you still hear the count up to ten to awaken you at the end of the track, you have probably been in a deep trance throughout. In this state you will still have absorbed all the suggestions on an unconscious level. If you don't hear the count up at the end, you have probably drifted into a deep sleep at some point. In this case you will absorb the suggestions only to the point where you went into a deeper sleep. If this happens, avoid listening when you are tired.

Hypnosis Scripts for Abundance

The following two scripts have been adapted from my CD, *Create Unlimited Financial Abundance*. Both scripts can be adapted and used for self-hypnosis or in a recording for personal use only. They are copyright protected and cannot be used for commercial recordings of any kind.

Script: Create Unlimited Financial Abundance

This script is very visual and places strong emphasis on financial success and material possession.

Introduction

This self-hypnosis script will help you create a very positive attitude towards money... and help you truly to believe that you can create unlimited financial abundance for yourself.... Belief is very powerful... the thoughts we manifest in our minds will become our realities... so you must accept on every level that you can create unlimited financial abundance for yourself now....

You will also need to take practical positive action.... For example if you've been struggling in a dead-end job that's limiting your potential... maybe look for a change of direction... or start a sideline with big potential... if something isn't working don't be afraid to change....

Induction

So close your eyes and relax... and open yourself up to the belief... that you deserve to be very wealthy indeed... very wealthy and successful...

accept this belief now.... If ever you were told you would never amount to much... or only other lucky people get rich... you can release any such negative thoughts... as you are going to create your own luck... just begin to breathe slowly and deeply and accept that you deserve all the good things life has to offer... and with each slow deep out-breath just feel yourself relaxing more and more.... breathing away any stresses and strains...

Now focus all your attention on your breathing... and begin to breathe slowly and deeply... in through your nose and out through your mouth... creating a circular breathing motion... and when you reach the top of your breath hold it for three seconds... then silently and mentally count to five on every out-breath... and as you breathe out you let go any nervous tension left in your body... and with each out-breath you relax more and more... and as you focus all your attention on your slow deep breathing... just let all your cares and worries go... with every out-breath... at this moment in time nothing matters... just allow this time for yourself... so that you can unwind completely... and go deeply inside and empower yourself

Visualisation therapy

And as you relax more and your creative mind becomes very open... imagine you are standing in front of your brand new dream car... you notice the bodywork is your favourite colour... and it is a top-of-the-range model... with a wonderful luxury interior... comfortable seats that support your body... electric windows... a fantastic sound system... with all the latest technology present in expensive new cars... you even notice that certain smell that new cars have... and you feel so good now as this is what you deserve....

Now imagine you are driving or being driven along... and you notice how comfortable and smooth the journey is... you love this feeling of travelling in style and comfort... and you accept that you deserve the best life can give you....

And after a while you arrive at your destination... your luxury dream house... which has been built to your personal specifications... your car enters the long driveway... and you gaze at the large garden... and you notice the tall elegant trees and beautiful shrubs and flowers... you pull up outside the large front door... and you take a deep breath and gaze at all the luxury around you... you know this is what you deserve... because you are very creative in thinking of new ways to make money... and once you get a new idea you always take action....

And as this thought sinks into your mind... you enter your dream home... and you feel very comfortable with your financial success... you love having so many beautifully decorated rooms... filled with everything you need and the best things money can buy... and as you journey around the house you soon come to a large conservatory... and there is a large comfortable chair in the middle of the room... you ease yourself into this chair... and lie back feeling very proud of yourself... for creating so much personal wealth... which enables you to do so much good... for yourself and others... and after a while you begin to drift off into a deep relaxing sleep... a dreamy drowsy sleep... a deep, deep sleep....

And as you drift off into this deep sleep your unconscious mind has become very open and receptive... and every positive suggestion... will sink so deeply into your unconscious mind... that you will be able to achieve anything you want to....

Post-hypnotic suggestions

From now on... you are going to become very motivated and determined... to improve the quality of your life... and you are going to create many new money-making ideas... and as soon as you get a great new idea... you will create a plan of action... and put that idea into action... and sustain it through to a fruitful conclusion... always making changes and adjustments wherever necessary... and you enjoy this journey... because you deserve to have a lot of money for yourself... and as you make more and more money... you become increasingly generous with yourself and others... creating an endless free flow of money towards you... which you happily spend to improve the quality of your life and that of others... and you love to share your success... and really enjoy the opportunity to create so much wealth... and to do much good with it....

And you always accept that you deserve... to have unlimited financial abundance... and to grow richer and wealthier all the time... and you always handle your success with dignity and modesty... and enjoy using your wealth to improve the quality of your life... and to help others....

Affirmations

And now... you can repeat some affirmations... and as you repeat them... say them with real feeling and belief... imagine every part of you... repeating the affirmations with complete conviction... draw these powerful phrases inside you...

I am always in the right place at the right time.

Abundance flows freely and naturally to me.

All of my needs are constantly met.

I deserve to be successful and prosperous.

I feel very comfortable making lots of money.

Allow your self-belief and determination to grow stronger... as all the positive suggestions sink into the unconscious part of your mind... and you will begin to respond to the suggestions unconsciously... in your day-to-day life... and as time goes by you will become more and more aware of the subtle changes in your life... as your attitude towards wealth and money becomes ever more positive....

And you continue to become... very motivated and determined... to raise the quality of your life... and generate lots of money for yourself....

Awakening

And in a few moments... slowly count up to ten... and with each number you come a little more awake... and when you reach the number eight... you open your eyes... and by the count of ten... you are fully wide-awake... and you will wake up feeling refreshed and relaxed... and feeling very positive and full of optimism for the future... as your creative mind continues to think of new ideas... to help you create wealth and abundance in your life... so as you count to eight... you open your eyes... and at the count of ten... you come fully wide awake... any feelings of heaviness or numbness will have left you... and you wake up with a feeling of wellbeing all over...

So ready now... *1... 2... 3* waking up... *4... 5... 6...* waking up... *7... 8...* open your eyes... *9... 10...* wide awake now....

This script has a strong emphasis on having a positive attitude towards abundance and wealth, creating opportunities and self-belief as well as financial success.

Script:
Develop A Positive Attitude Towards Money

The aim of this script is to help you overcome any blocks around being successful and prosperous and to help you focus on the fact that you live in a very abundant part of the world, and that you deserve to have some of that abundance for yourself.

When you put a good plan into action and you focus your mind on becoming abundant and create enough positive energy, you will raise your standard of living. How far you go depends on how much energy you create.

Induction

And so you can close your eyes and relax... and open yourself up to the belief... that you deserve to be very wealthy and prosperous... and that money always comes easily to you.... I want you to begin to accept this belief now.... If in the past you ever thought that money is hard to come by... you can release any such negative thoughts now... and accept that money comes easily to you now... just begin to breathe very slowly and deeply... and affirm that you open yourself up to new opportunities... and are willing to accept unlimited financial abundance for yourself on every level... and with each slow deep out-breath just feel your self relaxing more and more... breathing away any cares and worries....

As you focus all of your attention on your breathing... with every out-breath... you breathe away any nervous tension left in your body... and just relax more and more... and at this moment in time... nothing matters... just allow this special time for yourself... so that you can unwind completely... and go deeply inside and empower yourself... into the powerful and resourceful part of your mind... that holds the key to everything you want to achieve... your unconscious mind... which will naturally become more open and receptive as you continue... and you will be absorbing every positive learning deeply into your unconscious mind....

Deepening

Now I would like you to imagine... you are standing on a balcony... and there is a long set of stairs... leading down from the balcony... and the surroundings are very elegant and luxurious... the stairs are strong and wide... with a large handrail... going down to the bottom... and it is well lit... so you can see clearly... and in a few seconds in time... you can count down from ten to one... and with each descending number... you not only become more deeply relaxed... but you take a single step down... from the balcony... and with each step down... you will drift deeper into the trance... and when you reach step one... you can pause for a while... and wonder where you go next... you can then step off... into your own favourite place of relaxation... where you feel safe and secure... and at peace with yourself... and the world around you....

So ready... (create a 10 second gap in between each number... and feel yourself drifting deeper with each number)... *10... 9... 8... 7... 6... 5... 4... 3... 2... 1...*

Go deeper and deeper... into a deep, dreamy, relaxing sleep... a deep, deep sleep....

Therapy

But not the sleep of bedtime... this is a sleep where every positive suggestion... will sink deeply into the unconscious part of your mind... and have a lasting effect... and as you continue to drift... deeper relaxed... you become aware now... of a very positive feeling growing inside yourself... growing stronger all the time... a feeling that you can achieve anything you want to... when you focus your mind....

And in a moment... count up to three... and when you reach the number three... your mind will become very still and quiet... and you become ten times more deeply relaxed... down into another level of relaxation... beyond the one you are at now... and these positive feelings and beliefs... will grow ten times stronger... so ready... *1... 2... 3...* you are there now....

More deeply relaxed than you've been in a long time... every cell in your mind and body resonating positive energy now... and you know you can achieve anything you want to now.... and this feeling will remain with you... take a short while to enjoy these wonderful positive feelings....

SHORT PAUSE

Affirmations

And now... you can repeat these powerful affirmations... as though they are a reality right now... and as you repeat them... say them with real belief.... feel every part of you... repeating the affirmations with complete conviction... draw the words inside you now...

Money always comes easily to me now.

I see many opportunities in life.

I love and respect myself.

I create many opportunities for myself.

I deserve great success.

Post-hypnotic suggestions

And you will continue to believe... you can achieve anything you want to... and see more and more opportunities around you... and create many new money-making ideas... and as you think and feel more positively all the time... so abundance flows freely and naturally to you... and you often find you are in the right place at the right time... always meeting people who can help you... and when you communicate with other people... you express your ideas clearly and confidently... with great enthusiasm... and as you convey your positive thoughts and feelings to others... you attract other positive people towards you... and draw more and more opportunities into your life....

And as your attitude towards wealth and money becomes ever more positive... you are going to become very motivated and determined... to continually raise the quality of your life... because you deserve to be successful... and you love to do good things with your wealth... and share your success... and so it is easy for you to continually accept... that you deserve to have financial abundance... and to grow wealthier all the time....

Awakening

And so in a few moments in time slowly count up to ten... and with each number you come a little more awake... and when you reach the number eight... open your eyes... and by the count of ten... you will be fully wide awake... and you will wake up feeling refreshed and relaxed... and feeling very positive and optimistic about your future... in which money and success always comes easily to you... so as you count to eight... open your eyes... and at the count of ten... you come fully wide awake... any feelings of heaviness or numbness will have left you... and you wake up with a feeling of wellbeing all over....

Tips On Starting Your Own Business

Getting New Business Ideas

There are basically three things you can sell: products, knowledge or services. As previously explained on p.58 begin your search by focusing on things that you like and enjoy. Think of hobbies or things in your past that you have been good at or had a talent for. For example, if your big passion in life is playing golf, why not think about selling golf accessories and equipment. You will already have a lot of knowledge in this area as you have probably indulged in this pastime for years.

> *"The creation of something new is not accomplished in the intellect but by the play instinct acting from inner necessity. The creative mind plays with the objects it loves."*
>
> Carl Jung

If you feel that the accessories market is already overcrowded, look at the possibility of specialising in one type of product: for example, wholesaling the very latest new golf balls that are designed to fly further than before as the result of impressive new technology. If the wholesale margins are good and you market them well enough, you'll have golfers queuing up to buy them.

If you love classic films and have considerable knowledge in this area, perhaps you could begin to source new DVD versions of great films and sell them on-line or via magazines to a carefully targeted clientele. If you can buy at a good discount and sell around the same price as your competition, then you are in with a shout. If there is a big company already dominating the market, then market your business in a different way; perhaps by targeted leafleting or brochures, or offering a more personal service than the big company offers. You may have a talent for drawing, in which case why not draw unique pictures of celebrities, or special events, or places, and put them into nice frames and sell them?

If you are into DIY or interior design, and you have some savings, why not look at getting into the property market? I've always thought that property is a safe and easy way to make big bucks in times of boom *or* bust, as people will always need houses. Investing in stocks and shares, I'm not so sure about. Even the experts are often uncertain of which way the markets are going to move, so that gives the rest of us little or no chance.

> *"Lack of money is no obstacle. Lack of an idea is an obstacle."*
> Anon

My examples are basic and are not offered as failsafe advice, but they may help you to spark your own ideas of how you can draw upon your own talents. Whatever you start producing and creating you'll probably tweak and refine along the way so that it becomes more saleable. If you use the self-hypnosis guide on p.46 to connect with your creativity, you will come up with some great ideas for finding things you can market.

Before you go into the trance state ask yourself to bring ideas into your conscious thoughts, as all your truly great ideas lie deep inside your unconscious mind. This is where your true power and potential lie. Again the CD and the script for creativity will help you here.

The Internet

If you want to go the Internet route but you are a bit of a technophobe, then learn the basics of computing and setting up on-line businesses. Creating your own Internet website is probably the easiest and cheapest way to start a business in this day and age. It is not as complicated as it looks and you will learn as you go. If you are reluctant to go down this road, then find a techno whizz-kid who has the skills and consider employing them or offering them a percentage of your profit in exchange for free web design. Make sure you find someone with real knowledge as it is easy to design a fancy site but harder to make it commercially successful.

Marketing a commercial website is a totally different skill to designing one, and getting it right can be a steep learning curve. Once your site goes live on the World Wide Web, marketing companies may contact you, offering false guarantees of getting your site to a number one slot on a search engine such as Google. The Internet marketing tips given on page 116 will help you avoid some of these pitfalls.

If you don't go the Internet route, then you need to market your products or services either directly to the public through magazines or newspapers, or sell directly into stores at wholesale prices. You will need to create a good business plan and work out your expenses and margins carefully. It is also a good idea to put 25 per cent of all your income straight into a high interest account and forget about it until you get your end-of-year tax bill. You may not have a big tax bill initially as your expenses will usually take a big chunk of your start-up earnings, but it is good to develop the habit of putting money away so that you don't create a false economy. Remember the advice at the beginning of the book about not spending more than you earn? Well it is important when you start up a business as you are also collecting money for the taxman. Unfortunately there is no getting away from that.

Practicalities of Running a Business

This section is for those who have never started a business before, as it is important to get the basics right from the outset so that you don't get your accounts in a mess.

It is necessary to keep all receipts for absolutely everything you spend on setting up and running the business. Keep two lots of accounts: one spreadsheet detailing your sales and

> *"Money is better than poverty, if only for financial reasons."*
> Woody Allen

income, and another spreadsheet listing your costs and expenses – with all your receipts kept as proof of purchases. Once the money starts rolling in, you need to find a local accountant suitable for your size of business. If you keep your accounts in good shape, your accountant's fees will be lower.

Once your business grows you may decide to buy a dedicated accounts package. This can be a big learning curve in itself. Maybe by that time you can employ someone else to take care of your accounts so that you can be at your most effective while generating new sales and pushing the business forward. Delegating work is not always easy, but it is important if you want to take the business up to new levels. If you bring in good people in whom you have faith, it makes your job easier.

A Brief Guide to Setting Up and Marketing a Commercial Website

Please bear in mind that with the speedy evolution of website marketing some of this information will date fairly quickly.

Techno jargon

Domain Name or URL: This will be your website title, example:
www.golfballs.com

Keywords: These are a list of important words describing your products and site, for example: golf balls, quality golf balls, cheap golf balls, golf accessories etc.

Starting point

At the very outset you need to choose and then register a domain name that is suitable for your business. It helps if it includes your best keyword in the name, so begin by finding your most targeted keywords first. Start by collecting lists of targeted keywords preferably in two- three- and four-word phrases. Make sure that they are highly targeted and will only attract customers who are genuinely looking to buy products like yours. There is no point in paying for people to visit your site if they are not really interested in your products. So be clear about who your customers are and how they search for products.

Google and Overture are currently the two big players in pay-per-click advertising. Both companies have a tool on their websites that allows you to type in a keyword and find out how many searches they have had for that keyword. This allows you to find out how relevant your keywords are.

For example if you type in "golf balls" you will see the number of times this keyword has been searched for by users of the website and partner sites. Below this are other variations of this keyword, most of which are probably relevant, so filter the ones that are no good and copy the rest to a text folder and start your list.

Useful tip: Also list common misspellings, e.g. "golf bals".

I would suggest you find as many keywords as possible listing them in order of importance. You should aim to find hundreds of relevant keywords.

Choosing a domain name

You need to find a website that sells domain names, although you can buy a package from an Internet Service Provider (ISP) that includes a domain purchase. Domains are cheap at present and you should never pay more than £20 or $25 a year for a domain. The actual web space can be more expensive, especially if you are setting up an all-singing and all-dancing e-commerce website.

If your market is in the UK exclusively, then you really need a .co.uk domain. If you are targeting a worldwide audience, the best extension is the .com domain. Do your research and spend time choosing your domain wisely as it is not advisable to change it once the site starts to develop.

Designing and optimising a commercial website has become a highly skilled job so you would be wise to learn as much as you can about this. Make sure your site includes lots of useful free information and good relevant links both to and from your site, as the big search engines operate free listing algorithms that favour sites that are informative, and offer free downloads.

When searching for a website design company be careful as many will baffle you with BS. Look for a web design and marketing company who are helping independent businesses run profitable commercial websites. Always get references.

Marketing your site

Free listings
When you design the site make sure that all your best keywords are carefully placed throughout your site in text descriptions, links, and in the invisible html code. Once your site is optimised for the free listing search engines, you are ready to promote and market your site on the World Wide Web.

There have always been around ten to 20 main search engines and a million smaller ones that accept free listings. So find an up-to-date list of the top dozen search engines like Yahoo, Google, MSN etc, and add your url and website description to their free listing service. There are programs available that allow you to add your website listing to multiple search engines. One of the best is a program called Ad-Web produced by a company called Cyberspace. Once you have learnt the program it will save you a lot of time in advertising your site to the free listing search engines. After the initial set-up you click a single button in the program and it sends your site out to thousands of free listing sites.

Paid listings

As of 2005 Google and Overture are the only pay-per-click sites with which I spend my advertising budget to market my sites worldwide. They are partnered with most other big search engines, such as Yahoo and MSN, so my ads will be listed in the vast majority of important sites covering the web. Paid advertising set-ups are different in each case and require a steep learning curve.

Start with Google as, even though it is extremely complex, it is the most important site and has the potential to bring you the best returns. The best thing about this method of advertising is that you can start with a small budget to test the market and see which keywords work and which do not. You need to know where your market lies before you spend a fortune.

These are the url links to the Google and Overture advertiser programs:

www.adwords.google.com
www.content.overture.com

The main principle behind pay-per-click advertising is that the more you pay for a keyword, the higher up it will be visible in the paid listings. On the Google home page when you search for a product or service you will see many little ads appear in boxes to the right of the screen. These are the paid-for ads. The company that pays the most for any given keyword will have their ad listed at the top. The beauty of these commercial listings is that as soon as your site is ready and you pay to list your keywords, the ads become instantly visible. Conversely, the free listings can take years before your site is prominently listed. However free listings are still very worthwhile and should be pursued as a longer-term aim.

Further Resources

Further Listening

Glenn Harrold, *Create Unlimited Financial Abundance* (CD and Tape), Diviniti Publishing (1999).

Glenn Harrold, *Unleash Your True Potential* (CD and Tape), Diviniti Publishing (2002).

Further Reading

Dave Elman, *Hypnotherapy*, Westwood Publishing Company (1984). A classic on hypnosis first published in 1960 and still very relevant.

Sheila Ostrander and Lynn Schroder, *Superlearning 2000*, Souvenir Press Ltd (1996). Tips on learning and memory skills.

David Waxman, *Hartland's Medical & Dental Hypnosis*, Baillière Tindall (1988). A classic in the field of hypnotherapy.

Stuart Wilde, *The Trick To Money Is Having Some!*, Hay House (1995). A brilliant book on the metaphysics of creating financial abundance.

UK Hypnotherapy Courses

If you are interested in training to become a hypnotherapist, The London College of Clinical Hypnosis is one of the biggest and best in the UK. Their courses are comprehensive and offer in-depth training in the art of hypnotherapy.

The London College of Clinical Hypnosis
27 Gloucester Place
London
W1U 8HU

Telephone: +44 (0)20 7402 9037
Website: www.lcch.co.uk
Email: info@lcch.co.uk

Qualifying via the London College means you are eligible automatically for membership of The British Society of Clinical Hypnosis. The BSCH has centres all over the UK and the organisation ensures that training is of a high standard.

In my opinion the best way to learn and succeed in hypnotherapy is in a classroom setting with comprehensive training.

Self-help Products available from Diviniti Publishing Ltd

Hypnotherapy tapes
Hypnotherapy CDs
Hypnotherapy DVDs
Self-help books
Meditation CDs
Relaxation music CDs
Angel music CDs
Children's meditation CDs
Self-help DVDs
Relaxation DVDs

For an up-to-date list of titles contact:

Diviniti Publishing Ltd
P.O. Box 313
West Malling
Kent
ME19 5WE

Telephone:	+44(0)1732 220373
Fax:	+44(0)1732 220374
Email:	sales@hypnosisaudio.com

All the latest titles can be purchased on-line:
www.hypnosisaudio.com

Goals

_____

_____

_____

_____

_____

_____

_____

_____

_____

_____

_____

_____

_____

_____

_____

Affirmations